The Letter Book
Ideas for Teaching College English

Edited by

Sue Dinitz
and
Toby Fulwiler

with

Philip Baruth   Lisa Schnell
Mary Jane Dickerson   Traci Jersen
Jean Kiedaisch   William Stephany
Ghita Orth   Karen Stewart

Boynton/Cook Publishers
HEINEMANN
Portsmouth, NH

Boynton/Cook Publishers, Inc.
A subsidiary of Reed Elsevier Inc.
361 Hanover Street
Portsmouth, NH 03801–3912
www.boyntoncook.com

Offices and agents throughout the world

The author and publisher wish to thank those who have generously given permission to reprint borrowed material:

"This is Just to Say" by William Carlos Williams, from *Collected Poems: 1909–1939, Volume I.* Copyright © 1983 by New Directions Publishing Corp. Reprinted by permission of New Directions Publishing Corp.

"How It Is," copyright © 1978 by Maxine Kumin, from *Selected Poems 1960–1990* by Maxine Kumin. Reprinted by permission of W. W. Norton & Company, Inc.

Library of Congress Cataloging-in-Publication Data
The letter book : ideas for teaching college English / edited by Sue Dinitz and Toby Fulwiler.
    p.   cm.
   Includes bibliographical references.
   ISBN 0-86709-496-6 (acid-free paper)
   1. English philology—Study and teaching (Higher).   2. English language—Rhetoric—Study and teaching.   3. Letter writing—Study and teaching (Higher).   I. Dinitz, Sue.
II. Fulwiler, Toby, 1942–
PE66.L46   2000
420'.71'1—dc21   99-058139

Editor: Lisa Luedeke
Production coordinator: Sonja Chapman
Production service: Denise Botelho, Colophon
Cover design: Joni Doherty
Manufacturing: Louise Richardson

Printed in the United States of America on acid-free paper
04   03   02   01   00   DA   1 2 3 4 5

To Jeff and Laura,
without whom neither of us could have completed this project

Contents

Acknowledgments

We made the decision early on to make this book an inside job. That is, we know that instructors in disciplines other than English use letters in interesting and imaginative ways. And we know that English instructors at universities other than our own do the same. But we wanted to use the writing of this book as a way to bring together colleagues at the University of Vermont on a common project that would engage us in sharing our respective philosophies about teaching and writing, which is what this book represents. As editors, our deepest acknowledgment is to the community of Vermont-based authors who collaborated in writing these chapters by developing the ideas together, by responding to each other's drafts, and by revising in light of each other's suggestions. We also want to acknowledge the literally hundreds of Vermont students who wrote the letters on which each chapter is based. Finally, we want to acknowledge the encouragement, support, and helpful critique of our Boynton/Cook editor, Lisa Luedeke, who made publication of this project possible.

Introduction

Sue Dinitz and Toby Fulwiler

Letters are one of the most common forms of written communication in American culture, but one of the least common writing assignments in the academic world. The assigning of letters in college classes has generally been limited to helping students learn how to write specific types of letters: business letters, cover letters, query letters, letters to the editor. We would like to change that. As English instructors at the University of Vermont, we use letters in various ways to promote such things as classroom community, learning of content, experimental writing, and general literacy in our undergraduate and graduate classes.

The idea of using letters in the classroom is not new, especially to elementary and middle-school teachers. Many articles describe projects in which students write letters to pen pals at other schools (Lucey), to students in other grades (Stoneham), to their parents about books they both have read (Morris and Kaplan), to the authors of books they are reading (Arenstein, Tiedt), and to their teachers (Cox). Carolyn Linse recently published an entire book on using letters in grades K-6 to develop students' writing abilities. At the college level, one encounters an occasional talk at CCCC or NCTE on using letters: to solve problems encountered by a "real world writer" trying to teach writing (Addison), to exchange drafts and critiques with students at another school (Landis-Groom), to bring students into the community of writers (Ochse). And there is an occasional article on using letters in the composition classroom (Frye, Fulwiler) or the literature classroom (Taylor). In this book, we would like to look more closely and formally at how letters can be used for a variety of purposes across the English Studies college curriculum. We would like letters to start receiving the same attention accorded to journals as a tool for learning in undergraduate and graduate classes (as, for example, in *The Journal Book,* edited by Toby Fulwiler).

Why letters? Letter writing is as natural and easy as writing ever gets. Everyone knows how to write letters. Graduate students, undergraduates, and instructors have written, received, and read letters of one sort or another all their lives. Before reaching college, students saturate their classrooms with unassigned letters—called "notes"—with or without teacher approval. As college instructors, we can continue to take advantage of students' experience writing letters.

Letters can be helpful throughout the writing and learning process. The writing-across-the-curriculum movement has demonstrated how writing promotes learning. When people write about anything, they learn more about it—sometimes more than they expect. They learn about what they do know, what they don't know, and often what they need to find out next. Sometimes, writing that sets out to answer one set of questions ends up posing others. Serious writing is a dynamic, unpredictable thinking process, seldom in a straight line, seldom completed in a single attempt. Too many school assignments cut this complicated process short, asking that a draft answer old questions without raising new ones. By contrast, writing letters, like writing in journals, promotes a dialogical give and take between author and ideas. And when the teacher or fellow students write letters in response, other voices than the writer's can participate in this dialogue. In Chapter 9, Mary Jane Dickerson explores how the letters graduate students exchanged in dialogue groups evolved into their seminar papers and were featured in students' final portfolios documenting their learning. And in Chapter 1, Sue Dinitz looks at how responding to students' drafts through a letter exchange between student and teacher created a side conversation that encouraged students to extend their thinking about their draft and about the nature of reading and writing.

While letters can be tentative and exploratory, letter writers are usually trying to communicate something to somebody. Because letters usually have a clearly defined purpose and audience, the form often elicits focused, clear writing. Students sometimes produce dreadful academic papers, yet, as Wayne Booth notes in the opening to his essay "The Rhetorical Stance," these same students can produce coherent writing about the same academic subject in a letter because they approach this form with a clear sense of their rhetorical stance. In Chapter 3, Ghita Orth explores how this same phenomenon occurs when creative-writing students write letter poems.

Though written to somebody for a purpose, letters allow students to write without focusing strictly on matters of convention. When people write letters to those they trust, they tend to worry less about correctness and more about the matters on their minds. Letter writers don't try to make mistakes, but when they do no one cares much. By not worrying about correctness, students can focus on their ideas first. But lack of concern about correctness does not mean lack of concern about style. Writing letters can actually help students develop and exercise a range of voices. Most people write letters in a casual, informal voice similar to how they speak, using frequent first-person pronouns, contractions, personal asides, digressions, humor, slang, and expletives. Casual letter writers often prefer dashes to semicolons, ellipses to transitions, and sometimes use sentence fragments, other times endless sentences. Letters are a good and humanizing counter to the oft-requested objective voices of the academic world. They encourage academic playfulness—with conventions, with language, with readers. In Chapter 7, Traci Jersen shows how letters create a bridge for graduate students between their personal and academic voices, helping them develop an academic voice by allowing them to try it out in a nonthreatening environment.

Other chapters pursue this use of letters as a bridge from the known to the unknown. In Chapter 5, Philip Baruth shows how students in his eighteenth-century fiction class draw on their knowledge of e-mail to write their own epistolary fiction, which in turn helps them understand the form of the epistolary novel. In Chapter 4, Bill Stephany explains how, by writing their own "Letters from Hell," students in his Dante class recreate some aspect of Dante's vision in their own language, a process which helps them understand that vision, connect it to their own world, and raise questions for class discussion. While in a journal this use of the known as a bridge to the unknown would be a private endeavor, letters allow this exploration to be extended and supported through dialogue with other students and/or the instructor.

Letters can enrich the entire classroom by helping to create a learning community. By implying a degree of equality, letters can level the hierarchical nature of the classroom. Mary Jane Dickerson found that having the dialogue groups in her graduate seminar altered the relationship between students and teacher, turning her into a participant observer of the learning process rather than its director. And equality increases the likelihood of honesty; honest letters that explore teacher-student expectations and course content increase dialogue and encourage both student and teacher investment in the class, the teaching, and the learning. In Chapter 6, Toby Fulwiler shows how, by increasing the genuine sharing of ideas among students and teacher, collective letters written by the instructor help create a positive and trusting community of learners. And in Chapter 2, Karen Stewart explores how letters help students confront and diffuse cultural stereotypes that prevent them from becoming engaged with each other, the class, and their writing.

An atmosphere of trust is rarely enhanced by grading. Yet letters can add a new dimension to teachers' assessment of their students and of themselves. Letters provide an alternate mode—quite different from exams or formal papers—for assessing learning, and they provide a fuller picture of that learning. In letters, rather than being limited to answering the teacher's questions, students have an opportunity to show what they know. Letters provide instructors with a way to discover what learning is going on in their classrooms and to make adjustments to enhance it. In Chapter 10, Jean Kiedaisch demonstrates how a letter exchange not only helps tutors in the UVM Writing Center reflect on their tutoring practices and make connections between their reading, writing, and tutoring, but also helps her assess their tutoring, which in turn allows her to provide individualized mentoring.

Letters can shape not only the way students see the class but also the way they view learning itself. Letters encourage students to see learning not as a transference of knowledge from teacher to student but as a process. In a letter, students can start a dialogue with no necessarily right answer, conclusion, or end in sight. Letters are invitations to share, explore, query, and continue talking. Many of the recent scholars who have explored the nature of knowledge (e.g. Stanley Fish, Paulo Freire, Kenneth Bruffee) view knowledge as constructed through conversation within a community, and view education as enabling students to be aware of that community—to join in the conversation, to question it, to change it. While journals lend themselves to a view of knowledge as constructed by individuals pursuing their thoughts in scholarly isolation, letters correspond with the view of knowledge as socially constructed. By engaging students in the construction of knowledge through conversations within a community—conversations with their texts, scholars, classmates, teacher—letters are an ideal tool for helping students understand what it means to be part of a learning community. In Chapter 8, Lisa Scnell finds that in the process of exchanging letters about the course content, graduate students in her class on the Bible work out their own pressing concerns about what it means to be committed to an academic life, and if and how they want to make that commitment.

How can you use letters in your classroom? In the Afterword, Toby Fulwiler addresses questions and concerns about using letters, discusses techniques for assigning, managing, and assessing classroom letters, and offers some guidelines for instructors assigning letters for the first time.

The chapters in this book demonstrate a wide variety of ways in which letters can be used in the college classroom, just as the letter exchange itself can take so many different forms. In Chapters 1, 4, and 10, students exchange letters with the teacher. In Chapters 6 and 7, students write to the teacher, who responds to the whole group in a class letter. In Chapters 2, 8, and 9, students exchange letters with each other, and the teacher becomes an observer of, rather than participant in, this exchange. In Chapters 3 and 5, the letters become ends in themselves, with students writing them in order to create their own examples of literary-letter genres.

This multiplicity of formats serves a multiplicity of purposes. Letters can be places for students to reflect on and explore course material, whether that be assigned readings, their own writing, their past and present experiences related to the course material, or class activities and discussion. We see letters helping students develop their academic voices and identities, and helping turn pairs, groups, and whole classrooms of students into learning communities. Letters present opportunities for creative expression that in turn help students to become better poets and fiction writers and to better understand the craft of writing. And letters help not only students but also teachers—to understand their students, to plan classes, to assess learning.

You may be able to mix and match ideas from various chapters to develop your own ways of using letters, ways that fit your own style of teaching and your own purposes. After participating in our classroom sampler on letters at the 1999 CCCC, Clara O'Hara from Friends University sent us the following e-mail:

```
Just wanted to update you on how I used "letter" writ-
ing once I returned from the conference. I would have
to say that the response has been great from my stu-
dents. They much prefer letter writing to journal
writing. I kind of combined two ideas from the con-
```

ference. I had a Friday letter due each week, and from
that I found out specific problems students were having with the early drafts and assignments. Then I also
had them submit a short letter with their first drafts
about what specific areas they wanted me to look at in
their papers. I found that the students soon began to
validate and realize some problems that I had noticed
earlier in the semester with their papers. Our semester is winding down, but I definitely plan to use
letter writing as a weekly endeavor next fall.

As you try out some of our ideas and develop your own, please drop us a letter
(by post or e-mail) about your experiences and become part of our effort to explore how letters can support student writing and learning. Letters for any of
the authors can be sent to the Department of English, 400 Old Mill, University
of Vermont, Burlington, Vermont 05405, or to any of the following e-mail addresses: pbaruth@zoo.uvm.edu, mdickers@zoo.uvm.edu, sdinitz@zoo.uvm.
edu, tfulwile@zoo.uvm.edu, jkiedais@zoo.uvm.edu, gorth@zoo.uvm.edu,
lschnell@zoo.uvm.edu, tjersen@alexanderogilvy.com, stewartk@beloit.edu

Works Cited

Addison, E. 1991. "A Real-World Writer Reenters the Classroom." Conference on College Composition and Communication. Boston, MA.

Arenstein, M. 1977. "Traveling With Children Into the World of Books." *Language Arts*
54.8: 933–5.

Booth, W. 1963. "The Rhetorical Stance." *College Composition and Communication*
14.3: 139–45.

Cox, N. 1976. "Mrs. Cox Eats Minced Morsels." *English In Education* 10.3: 1–7.

Frye, B. 1989. "Artful Compositions, Corder's 'Laws of Composition,' and the Weekly
Letter: Two Approaches to Teaching Invention and Arrangement in Freshmen English." *Journal of Teaching Writing* 8.2: 1–14.

Fulwiler, T., ed. 1987. *The Journal Book*. Portsmouth, NH: Boynton/ Cook.

———. 1997. "Writing Back and Forth: Class Letters." In *Writing to Learn: Strategies
for Assigning and Responding to Writing Across the Disciplines,* eds. M.D. Sorcinelli and P. Elbow, 15–25. San Francisco: Jossey-Bass.

Landis-Groom, E. 1992. "Using Letters Between Classes and Campuses to Improve
Writing Skills." 82nd Annual Meeting of the National Council of Teachers of English. Louisville, Kentucky.

Linse, C. 1997. *The Treasured Mailbox: How to Use Authentic Correspondence With
Children, K-6*. Portsmouth, NH: Heinemann.

Lucey, W. 1986. "Learning Collaboratively—For Teachers Too." *Highway One* 9.3 : 47–9.

Morris, N. and I. Kaplan. 1994. "Middle School Parents Are Good Partners for Reading." *Journal of Reading* 38.2: 130–1.

Ochse, R. 1997. "The Pedagogy of Disclosure: Class Letters Fostering Partnerships Between Instructor and Students." Conference on College Composition and Communication. Phoenix, AZ.

Stoneham, J. 1986. "What Happens When Students Have a Real Audience?" *Journal of Teaching Writing* 5.2: 281–7.

Taylor, L. 1992. "Students Write Back: Letters in American Literature." *Teaching English in the Two-Year College.* 19.3: 201–5.

Tiedt, I. 1988. "Reading With a Writer's Eye." *Learning.* 16.7: 66–8.

1

Writing and Responding as Conversation in First-Year Composition

Sue Dinitz

```
Dear Sue,
    In Draft 3 I'm trying to see if the quote is strong
enough to stand alone. From here I'm not really sure
what else to do. I would like to see if you think the
quote can stand alone and what connection it makes.
I also want to know what role the tree plays in the
story. I still don't know how to put in how Greg made
me stronger. I see the paper turning more towards the
tree.

                                                 Rachel
```

Like most writing teachers, I spend much time outside of class responding to student papers. For the past few years, I've done this responding in the form of a letter exchange. On the day drafts are due, students write a letter like Rachel's, describing how they see their draft, what plans they have for the next draft, and what sorts of response they would like from me. Rather than writing comments directly on their paper, I write a response letter on the back of their letter.

Deciding to respond through letters reflected my interest in encouraging students in my first-year composition classes to view academic writing as part of a conversation. I wanted them to think of their papers not as isolated individual expressions but as part of a larger conversation taking place among other people and texts. As one of the textbooks for the course, I chose *The Presence of Others* (Lunsford and Ruszkiewicz), a collection of essays on subjects such as gender, education, science, difference, home, and work, deliberately chosen to create a conversation and invite students to join it. Responding to students' drafts in the form of a letter would, I felt, reinforce a view of their texts as part of a conversation that readers could join.

The letter form also reflected my interest in blending the personal and the academic in my first-year writing classes. Students began by constructing their own interpretation of a text of their choice. Though their paper was to be written as an argument supporting a thesis, I encouraged students to choose a text that helped them explore an issue or situation of interest to them, and to include an examination of their personal response to the text and its connection to their own experience when appropriate. Thus viewing reading as interpretive and grounded in the personal, we considered how writing can be thought of as an act of reading, in that writers are always "reading" their subject matter. Students went on to write an essay offering their interpretation of some aspect(s) of their own experience; an article conveying their reading of a person, place, event, or issue of interest or significance to them; and an introduction to their final portfolio reflecting on one or more of the stories it told about the student as writer. With this focus on integrating the personal and the academic, it made sense to make my responses to students' writing more personal by writing in the form of a letter.

This chapter examines how the letter exchange shaped my responding to student papers and helped me accomplish my goals for the class. I did not analyze the letters as we were exchanging them. At the end of the semester, I collected all of the letters the students had written to me and all of my letters back— over 400 in all—and studied the nature of the conversations we had had.

Writers' and Readers' Roles

One of my goals in a writing class is to help students become better readers of their own drafts, to help them develop the ability to see how early drafts, when reread, pose questions to the writer that allow meaning to unfold. I found that having students write a letter to me about their drafts encouraged them to engage in this type of reading. In the letter opening this chapter, Rachel was writing about an essay reflecting on her experience trying to comfort her friend Greg upon the death of his brother. She claimed she wasn't sure what else to do with her draft, but the rest of her letter suggests otherwise. She saw "the paper turning more towards the tree": for Rachel, the paper had taken on a life of its own, revealing what she wanted to think about further (the tree, the site of her conversation with Greg). It revealed where her ideas still weren't fully present in the writing (how Greg made her stronger). And she was not sure how well her opening quotation worked.

Rachel's letter also revealed how she had constructed me, her instructor, as her audience. Another of my goals is to help students see readers of their drafts not as experts who will tell them what to change but rather as interpreters whose responses can extend and enrich the conversations they have with their own texts. Rachel's letter constructed me as such a reader. She didn't ask me to tell her what to do with her text. Rather, she asked me to describe how I interpreted it—what connections I saw between her opening quotation and the text, what role I saw the tree playing, what her text suggested to me about Greg's effect on her. Rachel, then, could take my interpretations of her text and consider their implications for revision. In writing a letter back to Rachel, I accepted this role she had created for me:

> Dear Rachel,
>
>   I, too, see the tree as really central to the piece. For me, the tree first becomes alive with the memory of Pete, and then later Pete seems to be there, in the tree. As for the quote — I found that the part "Don't even try to understand/ Just find a place to make your stand" resonates well with the paper. But the "Lighten up while you still can . . . take it easy" doesn't resonate quite as well. You and Greg don't seem to be "taking it easy." Do you think this is Pete's message to you — in the embrace? And I don't get the part about Greg making you stronger? Perhaps more detail in the second scene would help? A really promising piece, Rachel!
>
>   Sue

But not all students in this class were like Rachel. I wasn't always willing to fulfill the role a student created for me. In fact, students' letters were often useful in what they revealed about how students were constructing themselves as writer and me as reader. Notice how differently Preston (writing about his quest to catch a giant trout) constructed our relationship:

> Dear Sue,
>
>   I feel like I am finished with this paper #2. I've been working on editing this paper and think that I've done all I can. I've corrected all the comments my group has given me as well as your comments. Feedback from you that would be useful is if you actually think I'm finished or not. If I'm not, in your point of view, commenting on what else I should do to this paper to make it a finished product will help me out greatly, because in my point of view I do not know what else I need to do.
>
>   Preston

Here Preston was not working very hard—or had not developed the ability—to see what his writing revealed. He wanted me to do that work. Readers (his group and I) were the experts who identified what was wrong with his paper so he could "correct" it, and it could become a finished product. Preston saw me as a certifier, certifying that a piece was finished or telling him what else to do.

Nancy Sommers (1982) has discussed how revision is hindered when "teachers' comments take students' attention away from their own purposes in writing a particular text and focus that attention on the teachers' purpose in commenting" (149); but some of my students were like Preston—they wanted me to take over control of their paper, not realizing that this hinders rather than supports revision. Rather than directly responding to Preston's letter, I tried to redirect his interest back into his paper and away from me, modeling different roles in the relationship between writer and reader/teacher:

> Dear Preston,
>
> I think there's still some work to do on pp. 2-3. On p. 2, I lose the time frame of the story. First your grandfather passes on the quest to you, then you're going out fishing, but after breaking your leg the first week of the summer. Is this all in the same summer? . . . How much you had the quest in mind when going out that morning also could be clearer. And I noted some places where you could still work on editing. This is such a good story that I'd like to see you reread, revise, and edit more thoughtfully and carefully. Don't just correct what I note; perfect the paper for yourself.
>
> Sue

I could have written these comments directly on Preston's paper, but the letter exchange allowed me to frame them as an attempt to change Preston's view of the nature of revision.

Reading and Writing Processes

Letters sometimes helped me peel back another layer, revealing how students viewed the act of reading. Porter wrote the following response to my letter on his research essay about the exploitation of college athletes (which he had submitted without a letter, so I had been unable to use his own thoughts as a context for responding):

> Dear Sue,
>
> Friday's group allowed me to get some good feedback. I thought I was getting really good feedback from my group. However, when I got back the copy you looked at, I realized I must not have gotten good feedback from the group. My group thought it was a good paper and that I had some minor changes to make.

```
You thought that I have mountains of work left and
that my organization was poor. If this is the case
then my group did not provide me with good feedback.
                                              Porter
```

Porter was annoyed that his group and his teacher read his paper so differently. And he implicitly suggested that one of us must be wrong. This letter alerted me to a conflict which I otherwise wouldn't have known about and provided me with an opportunity to have a class discussion of how we all were reading drafts—what process we each had gone through in responding to the papers and what we each had been looking for as we read. We discovered that many students had read through drafts quickly looking for things that stood out as problems, while I had spent quite a bit of time reading and analyzing each piece, thinking about what more the writer might do in the next draft. This discussion seemed to satisfy Porter and engaged the whole class in thinking about different ways of reading and how they are shaped by different purposes.

Letters also revealed how students were constructing the process of writing. For her first paper, Liz was inspired by Zora Neale Hurston's "How It Feels To Be Colored Me" to reflect on her own experience feeling like a minority when she had traveled in the Caribbean. About her first draft, Liz wrote:

```
Dear Sue,
     The group has not discussed my paper yet. I like
the topic of my paper but it is just hard for me to
organize. In the next draft I would like to have bet-
ter organization. The actual writing is not that bad
but the organization is awful. When you read the pa-
per could you please give me some tips on how to
organize.
                                         Thanks, Liz
```

It sounded as if somewhere Liz had gotten the notion that organizing is something that has to take place separately from "the actual writing." And I guessed her idea that she needed to have an organized first draft was probably inhibiting her writing and revising. Addressing this concept of the writing process was perhaps as helpful to Liz as any specific comments I could have made about her draft:

```
Dear Liz,
     I think it's helpful to not think about organiz-
ing at first — to just see what you have to say. In this
draft you've noted lots of the experiences and ideas
you want to work with. I still wouldn't worry much
about organizing in your next draft. Now that you've
gotten some of your ideas down on paper, you have the
```

> opportunity to explore (1) what exactly Hurston is
> saying about being in the minority; (2) what your own
> experience was; and (3) how these connect. Think about
> telling us what you experienced in a way that makes
> us experience it too, so that we'll really feel and
> understand what the experience made you realize. (I
> can't tell from this draft.) As I'm not sure you'll
> understand what I mean by this, perhaps we should
> meet and look at it together? If you'd like to do
> this, see me after class.
>
>   Sue

In what they revealed about students' constructions of reading/writing processes, letters allowed me to have discussions with students on larger conceptual levels rather than just focusing on what to do with their texts. And the letter form reinforced this discussion: it acknowledged the subjective, interpretive nature of the reading process by clearly identifying my response as *mine* rather than the response of some universal audience. Many composition theorists have called for writing teachers to apply what we know about the reading process to our reading of student texts. Bruce Lawson and Susan Sterr Ryan (1989) note that, "it does not yet seem to be the case that the developing awareness of the nature of text and reader-text relations has had significant impact on the way most teachers read and evaluate student texts" (xv). As Edward White (1994) explains: "After two decades of poststructural theory, we can no longer imagine that the text is a simple object or that our reading of it is somehow objective or neutral. We must be aware that the value of a text is negotiated, culture-bound, located in social structures. We come to student texts as we come to any other texts, out of our own positions as people of a particular class, color, gender, age, and background. We respond as sensitively as we can, and we must finally record our evaluations on grade sheets; but the arrogance, arbitrariness, and ethnocentricity of some teachers of the past might well be left behind along with their lessons in elocution and penmanship" (112–13). Letters help us convey this view of the reading process to our students. And Peter Elbow (n.d.) suggests that when we do present our responses as personal rather than as "universal truths," students find them more palatable (2).

So when John wrote an article on a boxing match, I didn't pretend to respond as a general authority on writing (or boxing). I acknowledged to John that

> Since I don't read or write this type of article, it's
> difficult for me to respond as your intended readers
> might. Perhaps it would help me and you if we looked
> at a few articles of the sort you'd like to write?
> Perhaps even check out some of the pieces written on
> this fight? Do you have other ideas for Draft 2? I'll
> try to talk with you during class.
>
>   Sue

And when I felt as if I had lost perspective on another student's paper, I could write, "Chalon, I, too, feel like I've read this piece so much that I can't read it as a 'fresh' reader would. I'm glad you're taking this to the Writing Center."

Letters encouraged other discussions at a conceptual level, as when, for example, they revealed students' notions about conventions. In the following letter accompanying an essay about how her worst enemy turned into her best friend, Liz revealed (in addition to her on-going concern about organization) her concept of writing as argument, and what, to her, that implied:

> Sue,
>
> This draft I feel is pretty complete as far as content. I may fix the ending and make it a little stronger. My group said that I just need to work on sentence organization. I also need to work on general organization. I would just like if you could tell me if I need to add more to prove the enemies/friends subject. I added two situations that I think make it more clear but I just wanted to know if anything else should be added.
>
> Liz

Liz brought to her piece a notion of argumentation as presenting a series of points that one "proves" with evidence. Once I understood this notion, I had an understanding of why Liz provided very little detail throughout her story— once she had offered a "proof," she felt it was time to move on to the next point. This gave me a way to explain to Liz why more detail would strengthen her argument:

> Liz,
>
> In your letter you ask if you "need to add more to prove the enemies/friends subject." It might help to think of an essay interpreting personal experience as different from a debate-type argument paper in the way you "prove" your point. In a personal experience essay, you don't prove a point through citing one example. You're trying to recreate the experiences for the reader, so that the reader will see in them what you do (in this case, how Emily turned into such a special friend). So, rather than asking yourself whether you need anything else to prove your point, ask whether there's anything you could add to the story to make it come to life more. (For example, more physical description of Emily?)
>
> Sue

Responding to Student Texts

While I looked for opportunities to talk with students on a conceptual level about the nature of reading and writing or about genres, I also talked with them directly about the text at hand. And I found that letters allowed me to respond to those texts more helpfully.

Letters allowed me to begin responding at the place where student writers currently were, creating a way into our discussion of their texts. For example, I was delighted to read Dan's letter accompanying his first draft of the semester:

```
Dear Sue,

    This paper is not done. I wrote one statement say-
ing that we need to not ask questions, and then at
the end I used the quote saying that we need to ask
"the right question." This is a contradiction. I also
don't like my ending quote anymore. I don't feel that
it sums it up as much as I thought when I typed it. I
really need to somehow rewrite this and better express
what I am trying to say. I need helpful comments.

                                                    Dan
```

By reading his own text carefully, Dan himself had identified places that could help him think through the ideas in his paper (a response to Anthony Brandt's "Do Kids Need Religion"). I could encourage him to work with these, and then could suggest another place where he might do more thinking:

```
Dan,

    You're doing exactly the type of thinking that
will lead to your next draft. Use what's here — what
contradictions have emerged — to work out more clearly
what you think. I think this is getting really in-
teresting — especially your observation that we need
to become more like children. In what ways do we need
to become like children, and why? Isn't there a quote
in the Bible that says something like this?

                                                    Sue
```

As in my response to Dan, the letters provided me with an opportunity to encourage writers to see their texts as connected to their own lives and to a larger conversation. When John explained how he saw himself as a "Wasichu" (a Sioux term meaning "he who takes the fat," described in Alice Walker's essay "Everything Is a Human Being"), I pushed him to consider the implications of this for his own life:

```
John,

    You say in your letter that your main idea is to
relate yourself to a Wasichu. This takes place mostly
```

in paragraphs 3 & 4. Do you want to do more with this?
You could explore both how you *are* a Wasichu, how,
according to the essay, you are responsible [for what
we've done to the environment], and what, according
to the essay, *you should do?* Are Walker's reasons for
why the Wasichu do this (which you discuss on p. 3)
your reasons? How so? What do you need to change about
the way *you* live? . . . Good work — keep going if you
want to!

                                                    Sue

When Bryan seemed more interested in technology than in scientific research
in his response to Lewis Thomas's "The Hazards of Science," I could help him
see his concerns as part of another conversation represented in *The Presence of
Others:*

Bryan,

    Is Thomas' essay about technology? Some of your
essay seems to focus on the application of research
rather than the research itself. If you really want to
focus on technology, you might check out the article
in your unit on Neo-Luddites? Or, make the relationship between research and technology clearer in your
essay? What does Thomas say about this relationship?

                                                    Sue

In his own letter accompanying his first draft of this essay, the ever-polite
Bryan revealed that he was using the draft to get all of his material out on paper, and knew that he now needed to work on shaping this material. Letters often pleased me because of this economy; I didn't have to tell students what they
already knew:

Dear Sue,

    While writing this draft, I discovered that I have
a lot of information that I have brought up to cover
and that it will be interesting to write this paper.
In the next draft, it would make sense for me to actually start organizing and composing the paper since
I only laid out points in no specific order on this
draft.

                                        Sincerely, Bryan

Without the letter, I might have told Bryan that he should start thinking about
the connections between his sections of material. To help him get started, I
even might have mentioned some of the connections I saw. But the letter
showed this wasn't necessary; I could just say "Go ahead—sounds like a good
plan," thereby certifying his judgment and encouraging his own authority.

Letters also allowed me to provide more focused responses by revealing why students revised as they did. The following three students all turned in drafts with only minor changes. If they had been unaccompanied by a letter, I might have written a general "annoyed" note back to each about what I was expecting. But look at the different reasons for their lack of revision:

```
(1)  Dear Sue,

    Here is Draft II of Paper #3. I changed some parts
around and added a little more "small details." I
spent two hours at the library on Monday night. Mar-
tha (the LUIS helper lady) wasn't there and the stu-
dent was of no help at all. I tried to get into ERIC
and it gave me 2 titles — but they were on microfiche,
and microfiche didn't have them on file!?! Then I just
went into LUIS and nothing of help or interest came up
except for 1 journal — which the B/H library doesn't
hold. So, I had no research to include.

                                                     Nia


(2)  Dear Sue,

    I really didn't do a good job revising my paper at
all. My intention was to write a whole new paper but
I'm still working on it. (I only have two pages com-
pleted.) I didn't get responses from my group members
so I don't know how they feel about my essay. It's
probably good, in a sense, because I will have a to-
tally new paper.

                                                     Dan


(3)  Dear Sue,

    I have not read my paper yet (to the group). I feel
good about the paper now that I made the changes.

                                                  Porter
```

In my letters back, I offered suggestions to Nia about library research, wrote a quick note to Dan to get his "real" revised draft to me as soon as possible, and directed my "annoyed" note to the student who deserved it, Porter:

```
Dear Porter,

    I would not consider this a revision. The only
thing you've done is add a couple of sentences?? Per-
haps you didn't understand what I meant by revision,
but I thought I did make it clear in class and in the
written assignment that you were to use draft 1 to
```

```
extend your thinking some how/way in draft 2. Do you
want to try again?
```

Sue

In describing their plans for revision, students often revealed their own views of their text. This prevented me from assuming that my interpretation of the text was also the writer's, from imposing my "ideal text" on the writer. Brannon and Knoblauch (1982) discuss how "adherence to an Ideal Text interferes with the ability to read student writing in ways that can best help writers to achieve their goals" (159). They point out how, when students lose "ownership" of their texts, "one consequence is often a diminishing of students' commitment to communicate ideas that they value and even a diminishing of the incentive to write" (159).

Notions of authorial intention and ownership of texts have been criticized as simplistic, intention being "under fire from theorists of writing because it distorts the nature of writing" (Crowley 1989, 99; see also Lawson and Ryan 1989, x–xv), and student ownership criticized as potentially "suppressing the value-laden, ideological, socially-situated responses that constitute constructive reading, thereby making the reader a mere adjunct to the act of writing" (Schwegler 1991, 220). Still, I find these concepts useful in my work with student writers. While writers might not ultimately "own" their texts, while the voices that go into creating those texts are not exclusively "theirs," while I may want to discuss with students the values implicit in their texts and the responses these evoke in me, I still want students to maintain control over their texts while they're creating them. When students stop trying to make meaning out of their own texts and start making changes just to please me, neither of us ends up very satisfied with the results. By responding to a student's letter about a draft rather than to the draft itself, I better position the student to keep control of that draft and to leave my class as a more confident, independent writer.

For example, Leah was writing a paper about her relationship with her much older boyfriend. She had described her first draft as "reading like a Harlequin, and it makes the reader think just as much." For her next draft, she had said, "I'm going to focus on the age factor, especially when I try to pass myself off as 18 and when we broke up." In that next draft, she assumed the persona of a grandmother and put the story in the frame of a conversation with her granddaughter about the granddaughter's boyfriend problems. When I read this draft, I couldn't find any letter from Leah, but I felt I knew enough about what she was trying to do to write the following response:

```
Dear Leah,

    Good for you!! You've finally told "the other
story" — the difficulties [of dating an older man].
And I like the conversation with your granddaughter
throughout — it adds an older perspective to the
story. I think the essay would be much stronger if
```

```
you included some more specifics — you remain on a
very general level! Specifics would make the story
"come alive" and would make it more meaningful. What
other people said about you, what your boss did, the
troubles you had — try describing these instead of
just mentioning them.

                                                    Sue
```

Then, further down in my stack of papers, I came across Leah's letter, which had been separated from her essay:

```
Dear Sue,

    I'm very finished with this paper. I really don't
like this draft. I don't like to dwell on the nega-
tive, which is really what this draft is all about.
It wasn't fun or as interesting to write as the other
drafts were, but was instead kind of tedious. As I
read through it last night, I realized this isn't re-
ally the type of experience that I like to remember
and therefore write about.

                                                   Leah
```

Leah's letter helped me understand why there was so little detail in her draft. It also prevented me from taking over Leah's paper and pushing it in a direction she had decided she did not want to pursue. I quickly wrote a new letter and then returned both to Leah, explaining what had happened. (Incidentally, Leah decided on her own to continue working with the draft that "dwelt on the negative," explaining in her next letter that "as I wrote, I realized that the only way to focus on the positive is to learn from your past mistakes . . . and once I realized that the story isn't negative, I really got into it.")

In a letter in her final portfolio, Rachel summed up how the letter exchange helped her keep herself at the center of her text: "I thought that these letters really helped. They made me get my ideas in order. I was able to focus on what I wanted to do. The responses that I received from you also allowed me to . . . make my papers the way I wanted them to be."

Indeed, it was sometimes in their letters rather than their papers that students stated most clearly what they conceived to be at the center of their texts, helping me get a firmer grasp of their purpose, helping me avoid constructing my own Ideal Text. In her third draft, Nia found a new center for her paper: rather than writing an argument about how to best "incorporate" students for whom English is a second language into her high school, she wanted to explore how, through working with ESL students as a member of the Student Council, she changed her own attitudes toward ESL students:

Dear Sue,

I feel "almost" finished with this paper. I tried to back up my research and show how my attitude towards the ESL students changed. I moved a lot around, cut out info, and added more of my own feelings. I decided my paper isn't about what the best way to incorporate these students is, but instead about — After working w/ these students, and understanding that they do need some specialized program — showing how my attitude changed towards the ESL students & program.

Nia

Nia never explicitly stated this change in focus in her paper, and the paper still contained parts of her argument about how to "incorporate" ESL students. Her letter helped me understand how she was thinking of her paper and so allowed me to offer more helpful and more concrete suggestions:

Dear Nia,

Wow!! Your changes have made this draft much better! *Your* ideas are now clearly expressed (what insights you gained about ESL students and programs). And your experiences help us understand how you reached these insights. I noted two sections of the paper (one paragraph on p. 2, two paragraphs on p. 6) that seem to be left from your previous idea for the paper. I don't think they belong, or that you need them, with your changed purpose. What do you think? If you take them out, you'll have to work on the connections between the previous and subsequent paragraphs. (If you don't see what I mean, I'll look at this with you.) I was really delighted with this draft! Whatever process you used in revising, try to use it for your other drafts.

Sue

Though I don't know for sure, I suspect that writing the letter offered Nia the occasion to verbalize for me and for herself what she was trying to do in her essay. In such cases, letters worked as "writing to learn"—the act of writing the letter led the writer to a clearer understanding of the piece or to the answer to a question or a problem encountered in writing or revising. In his second essay, Bryan described his reaction to a nearly fatal fall while skiing. Listen to Bryan thinking through in his letter a suggestion offered by a member of his writing group:

```
Sue,

    My group really didn't give me a lot of ideas on
my paper because they said they like it now. This was
obviously a great compliment to me at this time. One
of my group members did say to try and include some-
thing about my and Kevin's friendship and how good
friends we were beforehand. I wasn't sure what to do
with this, so I decided not to put it in this draft,
to get your opinion first. What do you think? Will it
detract from the paper because it's boring detail? I
am trying to focus on the adventure part, but I guess
it wouldn't hurt too much to have a small blurb about
our friendship in there. As long as the blurb doesn't
end up taking over the paper or leading the reader to
think that maybe that's what the paper will be about.
Anyway, if I did put it in, where would you suggest
I put it? Should it be in the introduction or in the
end when he grabs me and I end up calling him a "tried
and true" friend. I can't really slip something like
that in, in the middle of the action, can I? Please
let me know what you think.

                                               Bryan
```

Though Bryan kept asking what I thought, he talked himself through the possibilities, reaching the decision that it might work to put in a "small blurb" either in the introduction or in the ending. I ended up telling Bryan to try out both
possibilities and decide for himself.

In addition to providing an occasion to use language to think through their
papers, letters provided students with an outlet for expressing emotions that
had become tied up in the writing. Shiro, a student from Japan, wrote:

```
Professor Dinitz,

    I don't know where I am going with this paper. I
am tired and sick of school. Anyway, I want to write
about the different socioeconomic conditions which I
had an opportunity to see. I just want to write about
the socioeconomic gap in the U.S. Maybe you could tell
me or suggest to me what my focus should be after read-
ing my paper.

                                               Shiro
```

It may have helped Shiro to be able to say to someone not only that he felt lost
in his paper, but also that he was "tired and sick of school." Once this was said,
he seemed able to turn back to his paper and think about what it was he really
wanted to write about. He came up with the focus he asked me to suggest: the

socio-economic gap in the U.S. (which he noticed while volunteering in a high school in New York City).

Writing and Responding as Conversation

Responding to drafts through a letter exchange could be useful to any teacher who believes in the importance of revision in teaching writing: it encourages students to reflect on a draft, to verbalize their feelings and ideas, to think through plans for revision; it provides a helpful context for offering comments and suggestions; and it creates opportunities to discuss students' concepts of writers' and teachers' roles, processes of reading and writing, and conventions of various genres. In addition to doing all of the above, the letter exchanges supported my own specific goals by making explicit and concrete the notion that the act of writing can be viewed as a conversation carried on by the writer with his or her text, and as a conversation that is facilitated by other conversations with trusted readers and with other texts. These conversations, in turn, helped students see writing as connected to their own interests and the world around them.

The letters drew students into their papers, encouraging them to bring more of themselves into their writing, by having them, rather than me, look for the questions posed by the text, the places where more thinking could be done, the places where ideas could be brought to life. I could position my comments not as directions for revision that took the paper away from the writer but as a "side conversation" for helping the writer continue his or her own conversation. I could ask other questions, notice contradictions, point out additional avenues of thought, wonder about implications, suggest other texts the writer might investigate. And by presenting my response as subjective, the letter format implicitly encouraged students to get other responses (from their workshop groups, at the writing center, from friends and parents) to stimulate their conversation with their draft.

This view of readers' responses as enabling writers to have better conversations with their own texts was implicit in a letter by Rachel about her essay exploring the contrasts between her own daily life at boarding school and the daily life of a homeless woman in Collette Russell's "A Day in the Homeless Life":

```
Dear Sue,

     My paper still isn't done. I don't like how each
part goes. They seem like separate chunks of the pa-
per and not one whole piece. My conclusion, wait
hello, what conclusion? I don't have one. I tried to
write a new day in my life where I notice what I have
and I'm thankful for it, but that doesn't work. That
entire section is so annoying. I'm not proud of my pa-
per yet. It's not nearly done. I need help. Maybe a
```

```
conference would be a good idea. I know this was the
last draft for a while but I just can't stop think-
ing about this paper. Deb in the Learning Center (LD
office) helped me but it's still not done.
```

Rachel

When students can't stop thinking about their writing, when they see my role as helping them engage with their texts rather than directing the shaping of those texts, when they want to talk with other people about their texts, I feel like we've gotten to a place from which they can truly develop as writers.

Works Cited

Brannon, L., and C. H. Knoblauch. 1982. "On Students' Rights to Their Own Texts: A Model of Teacher Response." *College Composition and Communication* 33.2: 157–66.

Crowley, S. 1989. "On Intention in Student Texts." In *Encountering Student Texts: Interpretive Issues in Reading Student Writing,* eds. B. Lawson, S. Sterr Ryan, and W. Ross Winterowd, 99–110. Urbana, IL: NCTE.

Elbow, P. n.d. "Some Thoughts About Responding To Student Writing." Unpublished manuscript.

Lawson, B., and S. Sterr Ryan. 1989. Introduction: Interpretive Issues in Student Writing. In *Encountering Student Texts: Interpretive Issues in Reading Student Writing,* eds. B. Lawson, S. Sterr Ryan, and W. Ross Winterowd. Urbana, IL: National Council of Teachers of English.

Lunsford, A., and J. Ruszkiewicz. 1994. *The Presence of Others: Readings for Critical Thinking and Writing.* New York: St. Martin's Press

Schwegler, R. 1991. "The Politics of Reading Student Papers." In *The Politics of Writing Instruction: Postsecondary,* eds. R. Bullock and J. Trimbur, 203–25. Portsmouth, NH: Boynton/Cook.

Sommers, N. 1982. "Responding to Student Writing." *College Composition and Communication* 33.2: 148–56.

White, E. 1994. *Teaching and Assessing Writing.* 2nd ed. San Francisco, CA: Jossey-Bass Publishers.

2

Mailboxes Etc.

Creating Writing Communities by Exploring Cultural Stereotypes

Karen Stewart

```
Dear Karen,
     I am disgusted. That's all I have to say.
                                         Liz
```

I looked again at Liz's letter. Liz was from North Carolina. She had never seen snow until this winter. She had almost frostbitten her ears walking around campus without a hat—unaware that hats could be anything but a fashion accessory. She was probably tired and depressed because she wasn't acclimated to the weather, I thought, but I knew there was more to Liz's short, terse note than cold weather blues; she had finally articulated the general mood of this class—disgust.

In class, Liz and two other African-American students always sat together in a little group, separated from the other students by more than empty chairs and space. In another corner, members of the basketball team arranged chairs so that their long legs had plenty of room to stretch, and created another isolated group. Pairs of men and women sat in chairs so close together they appeared to be one, whispering. Several Japanese students consistently occupied three seats right inside the classroom door, carefully setting their book bags in the chairs around them as though setting out sandbags before a storm.

During the first half of the semester I had watched shy, tentative gestures of friendship turn into sullen silences. Students slumped into class. Writing groups were not working. Situation critical—or a teachable moment.

The class had just read Brent Staple's "'Just Walk on By': A Black Man Ponders His Power to Alter Public Space," and a surprisingly animated class discussion had followed over the effectiveness of Staple's dramatic opening paragraph:

My first victim was a woman — white, well-dressed, probably in her early 20's. I came upon her late one evening on a deserted street in Hyde Park, a relatively affluent neighborhood in an otherwise mean, impoverished section of Chicago. As I swung onto the avenue behind her, there seemed to be a discreet, uninflammatory distance between us. Not so. She cast back a worried glance. To her, the youngish black man — a broad six feet two inches with a beard billowing and billowing hair, both hands shoved into the pockets of a bulky military jacket — seemed menacingly close. Within seconds she disappeared into a cross street.

"It makes him seem like a murderer or a stalker," Sarah burst out.
"It sure does," Felix agreed. "It happens every day."
"No way," Tim responded.
"What do you think of Staples' use of 'thunk, thunk, thunk, thunk,'" I interjected, referring to Staple's description of the sound he heard every time he crossed a street in front of a car at a traffic light, as people "hammered" down their door locks.
"Oh yeah!" Felix nodded knowingly.
"What are you talking about?" Sarah looked bewildered. Felix shrugged and looked away.
"It happens to my brothers all the time," Liz volunteered and folded her arms across her chest.
"That's so rude," Victor said. "Why don't you do something about it?" Liz and Felix looked at one another, turned to look at Victor and shrugged. The room was silent.
After a brief homily about needing to discuss issues of cultural diversity in a safe space, which our class could provide, I suggested that students focus their weekly letters to me on their understanding of the term *multicultural,* and try to define themselves *culturally.* I told them they could not blow this assignment—that there was no correct answer. When I finished my comments, class was over and students began to head for the door.
"Good, I got lots to say about this topic," Felix stated emphatically.
"But I don't have any culture," Tim complained. I assured him that he did and asked him to give the assignment a try. Liz didn't say anything, but nodded her head, packed up her book bag and began to move toward the door. Sarah looked perplexed, sighed, and also packed up her gear. The other students rumbled and grumbled their way out the classroom door. I let out a sigh—I'd been holding my breath.

Letters as Journals

For several years I've used weekly letters as journals in composition classes of all kinds, and usually they work. When I explain weekly letters to students, I make sure they understand that unlike letters they write to their friends and family, these letters are public documents. I respond to weekly letters with a letter to the class, shared via an overhead projector, that includes quotations from student letters. I tell students that their names and words will be "in lights" unless they specify that a particular comment is not for use in open class.

I employ letters because they are a user-friendly form for student writers who have become accustomed to writing assignments they do not understand and often cannot complete successfully. In their letters, students can pose questions they might feel uncomfortable asking in class. Letters provide students with a genre that carries with it the assumption of a unique writing voice—the student's, not the instructor's. By their immediate validation of every student writer's voice, letters offer emerging college writers a site where their written voice is respected. For these reasons letters seemed an excellent choice for exploring cultural issues.

We had been using letters for several weeks, and I wondered why letter writing had not helped reduce the Balkanization in this class. Then I realized that very little writing, as Liz' brief note indicated, could take place while the walls of distrust and misunderstanding remained firmly in place between isolated groups, who were behaving like warring nations. I decided to read the prompted-letters defining *multicultural* and *cultural* and contemplate ways to use classroom correspondence to engage students in the task of getting to know and feel comfortable with one another.

In the following letters, six different students offer their definitions of *multicultural* and *cultural*. The letters are framed by a brief sketch that situates each student as I came to know and observe him or her within the classroom community. Within this context, these student letters established a starting point for discussions of multiple identities—ethnic and cultural, school and community, work and family. For example, Tim, a business major taking first-year composition because it was a requirement, reveals that he thinks others might disapprove of his cultural background.

```
Dear Karen,

    Multicultural means that the United States has
many different cultures. I was raised in a very slow
small town culture which is different than most cul-
tures. If you live in a city you have more chances to
meet many different kinds of people. I did not grow
up with different cultures, so I do not eat Chinese
food because I was unable to buy it at home. I guess
that makes me narrow minded.

                                                    Tim
```

Tim usually sat at the back of the room—somehow students still manage to create a *back* to a circle of chairs! He favored baseball hats, classic jeans (not the baggy bad-boy jeans), T-shirts with a variety of sayings emblazoned across their fronts and backs, and hiking boots. Tim seemed to be waiting for me to make composition "fun" and "easy." It was very clearly my job to do this, not his.

Taka, on the other hand, assumed that learning to write was primarily his responsibility, not mine. He seemed to feel quite comfortable defining *multicultural* and providing a specific example from his Japanese heritage.

Dear Karen,

    I'd like to write about multicultural and cultural. Multi means wide or many right? So multicultural consists of many different kinds of cultures such as arts, music, sports, and food. These cultures create a country. We can tell what each country looks like from their culture.

    For instance, one of the Japanese cultures is sumo. Sumo wrestlers express their emotions by fighting each other. This is my culture.

        Taka

Takahiro Kanno was from Nagano, Japan. While most of his classmates cheered the '98 Olympics, Taka wrote about being homesick and missing the mountains of his home. Taka wanted to learn to speak and write English clearly so that he could pursue a career in environmental studies. He was angry with his Japanese English teachers, who never spoke English and explained it to him in Japanese. He was eager for every English syllable.

Victor was also eager to acquire new language, though his reasons and Taka's differed. He saw opportunities to define *multicultural* within the individual.

Dear Karen,

    Multicultural to me means a person who has a number of different beliefs and behaviors throughout their lives. People who go out and experience new things or try new challenges are multicultural. A diehard country music fan who just decides to jump into a mosh pit just to try something new, is multicultural.

    I am multicultural because I hate being bored. Once I took a pile of rubber bands and made a tiny ball. I kept adding to it until it got to be the size of a small bowling ball.

    I hope this is ok because I didn't exactly look up the word "multicultural."

        Victor

```
P.S. A person who goes out and for no reason decides
to learn a foreign language, or see an opera, or just
exercise those old dendrites when they don't need to
is multicultural.
```

Victor worked at a local radio station as the board man who, according to Victor, "brings it all home." He had long hair, black plastic glasses, and liked to play with words. His reference to "dendrites" came from a short essay the class had read earlier: "How to Make Your Dendrites Grow and Grow," by Daniel Golden. Victor loved head-banger music: Metalica and Megadeath were a bit tame for him. He preferred groups like GWAR, who encourage audience participation of all kinds.

Felix was the only nontraditional student in the class. He seemed to embrace the "melting pot" definition of *multicultural,* but had some difficulty clearly articulating his complex ethnic heritage.

```
Dear Karen,

     What does multicultural mean to me? It is a blend
or mix of race, the ability to respect and enjoy oth-
ers differences — it's what America should be, like
the Statue of Liberty in New York City where every
race of people lives!
     I describe myself culturally as having the best of
both worlds — strong Puerto Rican roots, born a U.S.
citizen, able to live a free life — unlike our Cuban
brothers. I am proud of my African-Indian ancestry.

                                                Felix
```

Felix' employers had recently transferred him from Massachusetts to Vermont. His family had not relocated; he had found time lying heavily on his hands and decided to take some college courses. The first day of class, Felix wanted me to know that his writing was "really bad," but he was willing to work hard.

Sarah also worked hard, and like Felix, she seemed to have little difficulty defining *multicultural.* A quiet, shy person, Sarah's description of her ethnic heritage included a bit of everything with no clear connections between the items that she saw as defining her culturally.

```
Dear Karen,

1.  Multicultural means to me that you have many cul-
    tures living together. America is an example of
    this where we've incorporated all these ethnici-
    ties throughout the country. That is what makes
    our country so great.
2.  I would define myself as liking arts and crafts. I
    also like to go to the movies. My cultural her-
    itage is Scottish, Irish, French, Polish, and
```

```
Yankee. I am most Polish, which means my culture
originated in Poland. We eat gwumpkies and listen
to Polka Bob.
```

```
Sarah
```

Sarah had sandy blonde hair, a pleasant smile, and worked at Blockbuster Video. She had a difficult time writing a short paper on a catastrophe she had experienced as "nothing bad had ever happened" to her.

Liz' definition of *cultural* and *multicultural* moved from the personal to the general. Like Sarah, she included a broad range of personal cultural traditions, but unlike Sarah, Liz seemed to have a clearer sense of how the pieces of her ethnic background fit together.

```
Dear Karen,

    I believe that the cultural traits I have ac-
quired come from my ethnicity. I am half Puerto Rican
and half African-American. When my family has gather-
ings on each side of the family, you can see how dif-
ferently we react to each other: the diverse food,
dancing, clothing, and feelings and actions. Cultur-
ally I am a blend of all those patterns of actions and
feelings from both sides of my family. To me the term
"multicultural" means having several different kinds
of learned patterns of feelings, beliefs and actions
from experiences from other ethnic backgrounds.
```

```
Liz
```

Liz' definitions were the most complex of the six students' and it was easy to see some of the possible reasons for the frustration exhibited in her earlier letter. In her formal writing, Liz loved to use what she called, "poetic words, you know, the big classy ones," like "contemporaneous," "phantasmagorical," and "pertinacious." She was accustomed to being praised for her writing.

The Plan

After reading the class letters, I realized that students had always been asked to address their letters to me, and I wondered if altering the correspondent might alter the correspondence. I decided that maybe these students needed to write to one another—to establish a level of trust and a sense of comfort and community that was obviously lacking in the classroom. I thought they'd be surprised at how similar some of their views were and hoped that by increasing their comfort level, their confidence might grow, as people and as writers. I hoped that through frequent, ungraded letters to peers, their understanding of themselves and one another would encourage a writing fluency similar to their spoken conversations. I did not expect these classroom letters to produce great writing; I did hope the letters would break down the walls of silence between the mutually exclusive groups and promote trust and understanding, thus creating an environment where a writing community could flourish.

I made transparencies of six of their letters to share in the next class. Because I didn't want to inadvertently embarrass anyone or shut down correspondence before it began, I removed the names from the letters and assigned each a number. After we read them together in class, I asked students to select one overhead letter and use it to get them thinking and writing. Students were asked to address their response letters to "Dear Class," and to bring their letters to the next class. I told students I would provide the mailboxes; they would provide the mail.

Using a technique from Jeanne Henry's reading workshop, I set up a plastic milk crate with hanging files for each student's mail. I used student names on the files and covered each with a removable sticker bearing the number I had assigned that student, and brought the mailbox to the next class. As students shuffled through the door for class, I consulted my list and handed each one a slip of paper with the number of the student writer with whom they would correspond. These numbers corresponded to the sticker numbers on the hanging file mailboxes.

Students were asked to "mail their letters" in the numbered files and as they did so to peel away the numbered sticker to discover the name of their correspondent. There was some confusion, groaning, and a great deal of controlled tension as students mailed their letters. I recorded the existence of each letter with a check mark on my record sheet, and then invited students to "check their mail." Reluctant but curious, students plucked letters from the files with their names. Liz stuffed her letter into her book bag unopened, Tim quickly scanned the class to find the face that matched the name at the bottom of his letter and smiled hesitantly in that student's direction, and Felix called out, "Who is Victor?" I explained that each student must read and respond to the letter he or she had just received, by next class.

For the next four weeks, students mailed letters and checked their mail at the beginning of each class. I asked students to write at least two letters to their correspondence partner during the four weeks. After a student responded to a letter, the letter was filed in a folder with my name. I did not put these letters on the overhead, but I did keep a file of each student's letters which I planned to return to them at the end of the semester to use, along with their weekly letters to me, as raw material for a letter reflecting on their semester's work. I peeked at but did not comment on these letters.

Meanwhile in Class

In class, we worked on a paper about stereotyping. Each student selected a stereotype which *seemed* to fit him or her. They were asked to define the features of their stereotype and offer examples of how they fit and how they did not fit the stereotype. Students wrote about being short, blonde, teenagers, students, dumb jocks, Wonder Bread people and a variety of ethnicities: African-American, Hispanic, Polish, Irish, and Southern. In one student writing group, students discussed and commented on drafts with titles like "Memories of the Mall," "Blonde Doesn't Mean Bimbo," "White Equals Wonder Bread," and "Sports Smart."

Mailboxes Etc.

Here's a look at the correspondence between three letter-writing pairs: Tim and Taka, Victor and Felix, and Sarah and Liz. Taka's first letter was originally addressed to "#1," and is, as are all the first letters that follow, a response to the first overhead letter.

```
Dear Tim,

    I am from a small town too. It is in Japan. I never
thought of small towns as culture, I thought culture
was something from only one country like sumo.

                                                   Taka

P.S. I don't like Chinese food either. Do you like
Japanese food? It is very good for you.
```

Tim responded:

```
Dear Taka,

    I never knew they had small towns in Japan. I just
thought Japan and Tokyo were about the same. You
know, one island that was pretty much a city. I don't
know if I like Japanese food. Is it different than
Chinese?

                                                    Tim
```

Taka and Tim corresponded in detail about their favorite foods. Taka's letters were very persuasive with respect to the healthful benefits of Japanese food, and he convinced a reluctant Tim to drive thirty miles to the nearest Japanese restaurant. In his letters Tim worked to persuade Taka to include other students in their restaurant adventure, and was successful. The two wrote a collaborative essay about their experiences.

Victor and Felix' correspondence took a different path.

```
Dear Felix,

    I guess I really don't understand how you — a
Puerto Rican, African, Indian person can understand
me — I'm white. I don't have any multiculture — not
really you know? That's why I put the stuff about
```

music and moshing in my letter. I guess I don't understand what to do next.

                                                    Victor

Felix responded:

Dear Victor,

    What is a "dendrite" anyway? Like fake teeth? I
guess I could have mentioned that I like music — all
kinds — and I think music is cultural — you know? So
you have culture — it's not all about skin. It's about
what you believe and who you are. You are white, ok,
so what? You are free — guess what? Me too. You know
what I mean?

                                                     Felix

Victor and Felix' correspondence roamed all over the music world with occasional blunt comments about racial differences. When it came time to select
new writing groups, they asked to be in the same group. As Felix said, "I can
trust this guy. He always says it like it is."

By contrast, Liz and Sarah's correspondence was a bit tentative at first, as
Liz' response to Sarah's overhead letter reveals.

Dear Sarah,

    I like arts and crafts too, especially macrame.
Do you think we should write about arts and crafts
in these letters? What are gawumpkies?

                                                       Liz

Sarah responded:

Dear Liz,

    I thought that liking arts and crafts is kind of
cultural, but it might not be. I like African arts
and working with beads. I'm not very good at macrame.
Can you teach me sometime? Oh, gawumpkies are like
cabbage rolls filled with rice and chopped meat and
spices and cooked in tomato sauce. They're the best.

                                                     Sarah

Liz responded:

Dear Sarah,

    Sorry, but gawumpkies don't sound too good to me.
I like the special foods my mother makes for my birth-
day like sweet potato pie. Now that's the best! Who
is Polka Bob?

                                                       Liz

Sarah responded:

```
Dear Liz,

     Hi, how are you? Thanks for showing me how to make
that plant holder. It looks really cool swinging from
my window frame. Do you think res-life will be mad?
     You know what? We could have a dinner party. We
could cook at my friend's house off campus. What do
you think? Oh, and Polka Bob is this guy on the ra-
dio at home who plays nothing but Polish polkas. My
mom goes nuts over him.

                                               Sarah
```

Liz and Sarah did have a dinner party. Their correspondence was frequent, long, and detailed as they planned the event. They had no trouble at all planning a buffet of their favorite foods, but they had difficulty when it came to music. Sarah wanted some soft background music, but Liz referred to this as "Muzak" and wanted dance music. Their dilemma spilled over into conversations in class and soon the entire class was invited to dinner, and everyone was bringing a favorite CD—everything from the soundtrack from *Evita* to *MIB,* and even a tape of Polka Bob.

Students had no difficulty writing the required two letters and complained loudly when I stopped bringing the milk-crate mailbox to class. I was tempted to continue playing post office, but as I had to carry books and milk crate up and down several flights of steep stairs, I discontinued the practice. The letters seemed to have served their purpose. Although the class had not talked about the correspondence as a group, I had read all the letters and their contents indicated that the changes in the classroom atmosphere and dynamics were reflective of the informal, humorous, and respectful written voices in the letters. In class, students were engaged with one another and writing groups were humming.

What I Forgot

At the beginning of the semester, I'd encouraged students to use e-mail to send me their weekly letters. Students who did this received a quick individualized response, in addition to the opportunity to be included in my weekly response "letter in lights." I created an e-mail file for the class to facilitate updates on writing assignments and other pertinent information between class meetings. Students had not used e-mail often, and I'd used it less and less as I decided that this electronic form of communication didn't seem to work with this group of students.

I check my e-mail several times a day—ask anyone who knows me. One day, about three weeks after I'd stopped bringing the mailbox to class, I received a message from a student that read:

```
Dude,
    How are you doing? I just got your message and I
have no clue of who Lee Eldred is, ok? I guess this
means I owe you a pizza, right? because I know you're
just going to love telling me all about this guy. I'll
meet you in the snack bar at 4:30, ok?
                                                Victor
```

I was confused. This message was obviously not intended for me. I looked at the address and realized that Victor had sent a message using the e-mail batch-file address. The entire class had just received this message. I guessed that Victor had used the batch-file address by mistake, but I decided to respond.

```
Dear Victor,
    Thanks for your note. Is there enough pizza for
me too?
                                                Karen
```

The next day in class I asked Victor if he had checked his e-mail and he said, "Yeah, and I don't get it. I sent that message to Felix—at least I thought I did." Other students joined in the e-mail foul-up conversation, and I retreated to unburden myself of books and papers. As I laid out overheads and other teaching tools, I listened to the conversation and realized that students were still writing letters about cultural issues—not just run-of-the-mill e-mails.

When class started, I apologized for eavesdropping and asked them about their e-mail correspondence. "Oh, yeah," Tim said, "when you wouldn't bring the mailbox to class any more, me and Felix created a special e-mail file for the class. We send stuff to each other all the time."

"Sorry," Victor said sheepishly, "I must have responded to an old message from you by mistake." I was stunned. The writing community I had hoped to foster in the classroom had burst its walls and moved into cyberspace! We spent an intense class—I abandoned whatever plan I'd had—discussing their correspondence. In the end, Felix and Tim added me to their batch file. I seldom commented, but I read a lot and learned more.

What Did I Learn?

I learned that those students whose writing skills are weak and who often respond to writing assignments minimally, thinking they have nothing of value to say, have powerful things to teach; what's basic to basic writing is not the writers, it's the level of comfort, acceptance, and trust that must exist beneath and around language before any writing can take place. The building of this communal bond is foundational writing work. It may begin with a provoked student and a thoughtfully conceived writing assignment, but it only works to encourage writing if students take the assignment as their own, possess it and write from that newly developed place of security. Not a place I develop, it's a place they develop when they discover the pleasures of literacy for themselves in the written conversations of peer correspondence.

While students wrote letters exclusively to me, they had the opportunity to ask questions, reflect on their writing, and experiment with writing techniques—but they didn't. They wrote dutiful letters because they were required to, and their writing did not develop and expand in breadth; it dried up or stopped altogether—a reflection of the lack of dialogue and friendly conversation in the class.

What transformed this writing classroom from a site of intimidation to a site of exploration—a rich learning environment? Student correspondence offered a kind of protection through invisibility to vulnerable students in all Balkanized groups by permitting them to "speak" anonymously in those first numbered letters; anonymous student correspondence permitted students to begin dialogue. While student letters encouraged many features of oral conversation with which students were comfortable—regional dialects, idiosyncratic expressions, turn-taking, and individualized response—they did not permit interruption; every student was allowed to finish his or her written thought, unlike spoken dialogue where interruptions (and therefore misunderstandings) are frequent.

Peer correspondence also fostered a kind of "listening" as recipients could read and reread their letters before responding, ensuring a maximum understanding of each issue. Letter writers had the opportunity to revise what they had to say, making it more nearly what they wanted to say—something oral conversations do not allow. According to Roland Barthes (1977), this "possibility of revision distinguishes the written text from speech," and encourages revision as recursive processes or what Nancy Sommers (1980) refers to as "recurring activities." In peer correspondence the recurring activities of revision Barthes and Sommers refer to were prompted by the reflections of each writer and by the responses they received to their letters. These student writers felt more confident that their letters conveyed their ideas, thoughts, and feelings with a degree of accuracy not permitted when speaking face-to-face, because they could engage in a variety of revision strategies—re-"speaking," re-"hearing," rethinking, rewriting and responding.

As pieces of writing, the letters were filled with fragments—the written corollary to interruptions and clarifications in oral speech, but in letters the writers interrupted themselves and tried to clarify their own thoughts rather than being cut off by another speaker and denied the opportunity to reflect and revise. Letters were not grammatically perfect, and sometimes included tangents that took the correspondents into areas they had not planned to explore, which also reflects common speech habits. They offered the security of familiarity in an unfamiliar environment: writing. Student letters became both the initiators and the extensions of oral conversations in which students became engaged. Because letters were so user-friendly, students were tempted to use them on their own, and thus letters became a part of student writing processes.

As students familiarity with the letter form and with their peer audience grew, they explored topics they would never have touched in a formal paper. Student letters crossed cultural, class, and classroom boundaries in ways that more traditional writing did not.

The four weeks of assigned letter writing began a process that produced a variety of end-of-semester projects: a trip to a restaurant, musical discussions, and a dinner party. Odd results for a writing class perhaps, but events that strengthened social foundations and worked to create a tight community and the kind of support writers need to dare. Writing takes courage.

What About the Writing?

The letters, as written documents, functioned as extended experimental pre-writings to students' papers on stereotypes—and to subsequent papers. Students' writing did not improve mechanically, but developed in cohesiveness, variety and complexity. At the end of the semester, students still had a long way to go to master mechanics, but now they had their own writing to work with and could identify their particular patterns of error. They had begun.

I'd like to end with the reflective letter Tim wrote for his final portfolio and sent out via the e-mail batch file to share with the class. His letter—a fairly lengthy and detailed piece of writing—reflects his growth as both a person and as a writer.

Dear Karen,

Throughout the course of the semester, we have had to read different essays by different writers. As I have read these pieces, I have noticed most of these essays deal with minorities. At first, I did not enjoy these writings because I really hadn't read essays that covered minority topics. As I read more essays and wrote to students in this class, I slowly started to change my mind. The class discussions also changed my viewpoint. One essay in particular, the essay about Black language by Gloria Naylor. At first I hated it and thought it was ridiculous. It was rather close minded of me to think this language dumb. There are real differences between languages. These differences are just and understandable. I shouldn't have judged it on the way I was brought up, or because I never heard of Black English before. I feel the essays we have read and the e-mails I have written have made me a better person. They made me look from different points of view which I had never done before.

```
    Lastly, I want to thank you. I have really enjoyed
this semester. I have learned a lot about writing and
other things which will help me through the rest of
my life. Thanks again.

                                        Sincerely,
                                        Tim
```

Thank you, Tim.

Works Cited

Barthes, R. 1977. "Writers, Intellectuals, Teachers." In *Image-Music-Text,* 190–91. Trans. Stephen Heath. New York: Hill and Wang.

Golden, D. 1977. "How to Make Your Dendrites Grow and Grow." In *The Simon & Schuster Short Prose Reader,* eds. R. Funk, S. X. Day, and E. McMahan. Upper Saddle River, NJ: Prentice Hall.

Henry, J. 1995. *If Not Now: Developmental Readers in the College Classroom.* Portsmouth, NH: Boynton Cook.

Sommers, N. 1980. "Revision Strategies of Student Writers and Experienced Adult Writers." *College Composition and Communication* 31: 378–88.

Staples, B. 1997. "'Just Walk on By': A Black Man Ponders His Power to Alter Public Space." In *The Simon & Schuster Short Prose Reader,* eds. R. Funk, S. X. Day, and E. McMahan. Upper Saddle River, NJ: Prentice Hall.

3

"This Is Just to Say"

Letter Poems in a Creative Writing Class

Ghita Orth

I have eaten
the plums
that were in
the icebox

and which
you were probably
saving for breakfast

Forgive me
they were delicious
so sweet
and so cold

W. C. Williams

William Carlos Williams' much-anthologized "This Is Just to Say" is, in its minimalist way, a paradigm of a letter poem: it is directed to a specific "you," it is driven by the speaker's need to tell something to this individual audience, and it focuses concretely on the circumstances that have created such a need. In this case too, it seems the speaker has made a discovery about the experience, and his relation to it, in the process of writing about it. Although ostensibly an apology, Williams' "letter" reveals in the language of its last three lines that the speaker's pleasure in savoring the purloined plums may well outweigh the guilt he nominally expresses. "This Is Just to Say," in its other-directedness, its energetic immediacy, its dependence on images, and its arrival at a place the writer may not have expected, is characteristic of a letter poem. These qualities demonstrate why writing letter poems is a valuable experience for student writers.

Although Williams' poem was an actual note to his wife, as he acknowledged in an interview (*Interviews with William Carlos Williams,* ed. Linda W. Wagner, [1976]), the assignment I give my students in Advanced Poetry Writing asks them to approach the letter poem as an exercise—to assume its rhetorical stance rather than produce a literal communication to be mailed, or left out on the kitchen table. Some of my students said they would be willing to show such poems to their intended recipients; Laurie thought "they are great mediums to tell someone something that I can't just come out and say."[1] Others, however, agreed with Andrew, who explained, "The problems I talk about are ones I haven't been able to confront the person about—having them read my letter poem would mean a confrontation." Instead, writing the letter poem allowed Andrew, and others who shared his feelings, to confront the "problems" instead of the person—to investigate issues that might otherwise have remained unexamined and unexpressed.

Because they did not have to consider their "letters" part of an actual correspondence, the students were free to write to recipients alive or dead, close at hand or distant. I asked only that their letter poems be addressed to *people,* unlike poems of apostrophe which can be directed to inanimate objects, ideas, heavenly bodies, fauna, or flora. Although a letter poem is itself a monologue, it is implicitly part of a conversation, half of a potential dialogue; as such, it requires a human recipient as its nominal audience. A letter poem talks *to* someone—a "you" whose imagined presence in the poem makes direct communication possible, indeed, necessary.

The students in English 119 could choose any kind of format for these "dialogues of one." They could even employ the conventional salutations and closings of actual letters, as Richard Hugo does in the poems of *31 Letters and 13 Dreams,* in which, for example, "Letter to Bell From Missoula" begins "Dear Marvin," and concludes, "I think of you and Dorothy. Stay well. Love, Dick." Most class members, though, agreed with Laurie's view that "a letter poem is effective in containing some kind of personal disclosure to another person. I don't think it needs to have an actual 'letter' form."

But as a poem, it does need to have *some* kind of considered form. Writing about the making of his letter poems in one of them ("Letter to Berg From Missoula"), Hugo explains: "Usually, I took a fourteen-syllable line, propped it up here and there with an anapest, / and fired away. . . ." In English 119 some students cast their work in closed forms—blank verse, a sestina—and others chose free verse, but all were clearly letter *poems,* linearly crafted objects.

There is a long historical precedent for epistolary verse, from the Roman poet Horace's *Epistles* to the present; my students had access to many models of such poems in one of our texts, *Contemporary American Poetry* (ed. A. Poulin, Jr., [1996]). This anthology contains works by Robert Hass, William Stafford, Li-Young Lee, Denise Levertov, and many others which served as examples, demonstrating a variety of occasions for, and recipients of, letter poems.[2] Anne Sexton, for instance, writes in response to a friend in "With Mercy for the Greedy," which begins, "Concerning your letter in which you ask/ me to call a priest . . ." and Marge Piercy's "You Ask Why Sometimes I Say Stop" has also been occasioned by the need to *answer* someone, in this case a lover. There are letter poems in the anthology that are written to family members in attempts to resolve issues with them; Carolyn Kizer speaks intimately to her daughter in a section of "The Blessing," and Frank O'Hara asks parental forgiveness in "To My Dead Father."

Maxine Kumin's "How It Is" also directly addresses the dead, her "old friend" Anne Sexton, as a way of describing, and thus understanding, her grief:

Shall I say how it is in your clothes?
A month after your death I wear your blue jacket.
The dog at the center of my life recognizes
you've come to visit, he's ecstatic.

The need to talk to another when actual dialogue is impossible also drives Gwendolyn Brooks' "the mother." "Abortions will not let you forget," the speaker acknowledges: "I have heard in the voices of the wind the voices of my dim killed children." The poem itself gives moving voice to her complex response, provides her side of a conversation with these lost children that could only happen on the page.

It is this aspect of the letter poem—its function as written conversation directed to a specific person outside the self—that creates its most important challenge for student poets. The work of beginning writers is often primarily self-referential; in it, they essentially talk to themselves about themselves, "expressing" their feelings rather than attempting to communicate them to someone outside their private, personally allusive worlds and thus leaving the reader unengaged by the poem's circumstance or emotion. The letter poem, however, is addressed to a specific "other"; its intended recipient is a silent partner in the poem's implicit dialogue. Considerations of that silent presence can lead students to a valuable awareness of audience. For example, Hillery liked writing such poems because, as she explained, "I like writing *personally* to someone— without someone on the other end of my poem, I feel I am speaking to an empty space." An "empty space" can be the receptacle for any amount of diffuse material that writers may call up—whatever comes into their minds, or lives, at the time of writing. Letter poems, however, necessitate a "someone on the other end" who, the writer knows, would not have an interest in, or patience for, listening to generalized musings.

Not surprisingly, therefore, "focus" is the word that appeared most often in my students' responses to a question about what they had found helpful about writing letter poems. "My material was much more direct in my letter poem," Brian said. "Because I had a direct focus (the person to whom it was addressed) I was able to speak clearly of the circumstances and my feelings at the time to a known person." Jennifer agreed: "By placing the material into a 'letter' I had to address a specific 'you.' This, for one, kept me focused and clear."

And members of our class had no difficulty in finding specific "yous" they wanted to address. Many students seemed to be initiating dialogues around un-resolved issues of long standing, and for once, none indicated problems in find-ing something to write about. The letter poem, after all, creates its own occa-sion—by its nature it is need-driven. It benefits from the emotional directness and immediacy of a circumstance in which the poet feels compelled to speak, and students benefit from discovering the vitality and power such energy can give their work. As Adam noted, letter poems have "a *real* physical purpose. Not all poems are created in such a substantial manner." Jennifer said they lead writ-ers to "confront real issues that are, no doubt, loaded with emotions/memo-ries," and Laurie felt, "Addressing someone in particular helps me to really en-counter what I'm feeling." "Letter poems," Hillery concluded, "are really the best when the *moment* is right. When someone really has something (urgent?) to say to someone else."

These students' emphasis on the sense of reality engendered by a letter poem's inherent occasion suggests another reason why writing such a poem is a valuable exercise—it leads poets into a direct confrontation with, or discov-ery of, the sometimes hard truths of their own experience. The unexamined life has no more place in a letter poem than in an actual letter. Members of my class were willing to take on such confrontations, to examine their feelings and ex-periences in order to communicate them to the "you" their poems addressed.

Since in a letter poem especially there would be no point in students writ-ing only what they already know, what has already been said to their letters' re-cipients, many ventured into territory as yet unspoken or unconsidered and found this process liberating; they welcomed the letter poem's intrinsic poten-tial for discovery. As Jennifer saw it, writing such a poem presented the op-portunity for "exploring areas in relationships that one might not have thought to do before. When exploring these areas one crosses new paths on a well-known trail."

The invigorating exploration that a letter poem often requires of its writer led many class members to write their strongest, and truest, poems of the se-mester in this rhetorical mode. Adam acknowledged the advantage of "voicing those thoughts you may not otherwise say or even admit," and Emily said, "I found myself working to sort out my feelings for the other person, allowing me to speak to him effectively. . . . I realized the intensity of my emotions to-ward him." Charity put it succinctly—she knew her letter poems differed from her other work in the class because in them she was "more honest and less beautiful."

But in many writing situations, truth *is* beauty. One of Charity's letter po-ems, "Seventeen," for example, addresses a step-mother with whom the speaker clearly has had a troubled relationship and evokes the effect of that relationship on her ways of living in the world. In the poem's final stanza, however, its fo-cus suddenly veers from that subject to the emotionally fraught issue that is re-ally at the poem's center:

Leaving home
when I was seventeen,
I recovered by growing
into a hundred-foot priestess
in my heart.
Now every time something hurts me
I just keep growing.
Maybe one day
you'll cower in the shadow
of my little toe,
and Dad will love me then.

The poignant and surprising turn of the last line here supports Charity's assertion that "writing a letter poem to someone with no intention of giving them the
poem is empowering and healing." But writing such poems is not mere personal therapy. As in "Seventeen," the writer's awareness of the recipient's imagined presence across the page directs the poem outward, beyond self-pity or
self-indulgence.

One potential pitfall in making a letter poem, however, is allowing the conversation it implies to become too reiterative, too heavily expository, thus seem-
ing to remind the recipient what he or she surely must know. In Andrew's poem
"Fortress," the speaker tells his widowed mother, "We had six years together,
you and me," and, "of course you are hesitant / to enter into a relationship."
Since it is unlikely that the speaker must tell his mother what she is no doubt
already aware of, Andrew's description of her behavior is not what his letter
"needs" to say to her. But then he reiterates her situation in metaphorical terms:

You have constructed a fortress around you
with no gate, no door, impenetrable to anyone
who might attempt to trespass.

The poem now begins to move toward its true purpose, a discovery revelation
that becomes clear in the final stanza: "I have modeled my kingdom / after the
only model I have known. / I am my mother's son." Here the poem comes alive,
driven by the speaker's wariness of being similarly fortress-bound and his need
to communicate this to his mother, probably for the first time. The poem has
discovered, and revealed, what it is really "about."

In his inclusion of much information that would not *be* information to the
poem's nominal recipient, however, Andrew is responding to another exigency
of the letter poem. As he explained, "There are often problems in writing about
experiences shared only by the author and the intended person that confuse and
leave out the reader." To avoid such confusion, he had turned to direct exposition, for as all my students were aware, although addressed to a specific audience the letter poem is also going to be read by a larger group, even if only
the other members of one's writing workshop. Letter poems are thus "private"

communications that are meant to be overheard; these are letters that will be steamed open by others than the addressee.

Although, as we've seen, it serves the writers' purposes to imagine their letter poems as directed to a single known individual, there is a second, general audience for their work that requires consideration. Brian said, "My first priority in the poem was to speak to one person and not the ambiguous 'reader'. This helped me tighten my thoughts and feelings and let me be more at ease showing rage, fear, anger, and my own weakness in the poem without worrying what the 'readers' would think of me." These eavesdropping "readers," however, are out there, especially in a writing class, and the need to consider them in the process of writing a letter poem creates advantageous problems; in having to find effective means of allowing an outsider to understand and respond to a "private" conversation, poets must move away from abstractions, easy generalizations, and personal allusions toward accessibility. Learning fully to utilize concrete images, resonant specifics, and details that count strengthens their poem-making skills. Because writers of letter poems must avoid flat exposition while clarifying what the letter's writer and its recipient know without saying, they are challenged to develop those aspects of their craft that allow poetry to communicate most effectively.

Student poets may not always realize that what is entirely apparent to *them* may need clarification for others. They know, for example, to whom they are writing their letter poems, and thus may assume we will too, but this isn't always the case; they will need to build that information into the poem itself. But *is* it really necessary, they sometimes ask, for the outside reader to know who is being addressed in the poem? The answer is yes, for unless we know the identity of the "you" and thus understand something of the speaker's relation to the letter's recipient, we cannot fully understand the weight and import of the poem's dialogue or share its significance for the speaker.

Jennifer's letter poem, "Family Art," for instance, centers on two differing ways of looking at the world. An accomplished photographer in black and white, Jennifer addresses a "you" who paints oils in "vibrant oranges / and purples." She wonders whether this person could ever share her vision, could "picture the world in / black and white" as she does. Even in its draft version, the poem's central issue was clear to readers, but the significance of its ultimate question—what may be *at stake* for the speaker here—was not. Recognizing this, in revising her poem Jennifer added a subtitle, "for my father," and a line that referred to their signing their dissimilar pictures with a shared last name; with these additions, the entire poem gained heft and import for its general readers.

Many students used titles or subtitles to name or otherwise identify their poems' specific audiences; others made relationships clear through direct address, as in Hillery's line, "Mother, mother. It is never over," or implied them through the poem's details or even its organizational strategy. The first stanza of Abigail's "Undertow," for example, ends with a dream image in which "You sank, lazily, out of reach"; the second stanza begins with the recognition "Lovers are losing each other all around us," in a juxtaposition that clarifies the "you" as lover.

Other potential difficulties were not so easily dealt with, and often required students to re-think their initial approach to their material through a series of revisions. The three versions of Emily's "To Rob" demonstrated an effective progression toward clarity and concreteness that serves the poem well. Comprised of a series of real and rhetorical questions to Rob, a young suicide, the poem reflects the speaker's attempt to understand and come to terms with his incomprehensible act. The first draft begins: "Did you do it all / or even half / before you killed yourself?" The speaker's perplexity is real, but so is the reader's—who *is* Rob in relation to her? What was the "all" he may have wanted to accomplish in his life? Why does the speaker feel this compulsion to know?

In the poem's second draft, Emily clearly recognizes the necessity for concrete detail and specific references to orient the reader in the situation, and the poem now opens with vivid immediacy: "Cousin / I only remember being young with you." We now know who Rob is, and, by implication, why the speaker needs so much to talk to him. Similarly, a generalized reference to Rob's "future plans" in the first draft is here recast in specific terms: "You were going to get off all the medications, / be happy on your own." The reader can now begin to *know* Rob, to care about him with the speaker.

There were still places in the poem, though, that cried out for the images that could allow readers to share the speaker's sense of loss. "Did you make / the memories / so that we would have them?" the speaker asks. Rob would have known what "memories" she refers to, but the reader doesn't, not until the poem's final draft in which images of shared childhood experiences—a trip to an amusement park, teasing games, a girlish crush—animate the poem. Here, too, the speaker comes to a new and poignant recognition: "Once we grew and the family dispersed, / it seemed we only saw each other at funerals."

In the final version of "To Rob," twice as long as the original draft, such added details make him and the relationship accessible to a reader who can now be a participant in the poem's experience. All three versions of the poem conclude with the same rhetorical questions:

Am I supposed to think
you wanted this planned death?

Then, why do I feel you've been murdered?

Although "To Rob" still does not, ultimately cannot, provide answers to these questions, Emily's revising process has given the questions themselves a poignant resonance. The poem has grown from a generalized private meditation to a moving, and troubling, colloquy with someone the reader has come to care about, and, like the speaker, wants to understand.

In English 119 the revising process is where *actual* letters come into play—and not only in the revision of letter poems. In my class, all students, as well as the instructor, read and make written comments on their fellow poets' drafts; these comments, along with workshop discussions, help writers make choices in revision that can, as in Emily's case, immeasurably strengthen their poems. The letter poems my students wrote, then, not only helped them define a specific audience and accommodate the needs of a larger one, but also elicited actual notes from their peers, often begun with a salutation, and couched, as mine usually are, as questions—initiating a written interchange to which the revised poems are a response.

This literal correspondence between writer and reader added another level of dialogue to the letter-poem assignment, and further expanded its learning potential for the students. Asked what could be discovered about the ways letter poems work best by reading and commenting on peers' drafts, Melissa said, "It's the sensitivity of the specifics that come out without skirting the issue. . . . We are able to see the dynamics of the relationships," and Charity noted that "little truths come out in the form of great details."

It was almost always in the interest of clarifying such specifics and details that students wrote their "letters" on each other's drafts. For example, in the first draft of her poem "Seventeen," mentioned earlier, Charity had intended to make the recipient's identity clear through implicit internal evidence. The poem began:

> Leaving home
> when I was seventeen,
> I remembered when Dad
> married you;
> you were a child, still,
> at thirty-three.
> If only I had been as wise then
> as I was at seventeen—
> leaving home,
> taking back my spirit,
> immune to the words you hit me with . . .

This opening, though, led some students to question who, exactly, the person being addressed was, and thus to wonder what the poem was "about," especially considering that ironically revelatory assertion in the poem's final line: "And Dad will love me then."

Reading the notes her classmates wrote on this draft, Charity came to re-see the poem from an outsider's perspective—she had included details, but they weren't yet entirely clear to others. Melissa wrote next to line 4, "Not your natural Mom, right?", Brian noted, "It seems as if she is running away from family (step-mom?)," and Andrew asked, "Why does the narrator wish to hide from her mother?" Not being certain *who* was involved here, some students were uncertain of *what* was involved; at the end of Charity's opening stanza, Andrew wrote, "I don't get what's going on here," and Laurie was similarly puzzled by the poem's conclusion: "You are speaking to your Mom who 'hit you with words,' but suddenly the emotion is displaced by these negative Dad feelings. Where do they come from?" Charity had to find a way of making it completely clear that the poem was addressed to a problematic step-mother, who had married into the speaker's life, brought there by her father.

After reading these "letters" from her classmates, Charity responded to their questions not in an answering letter but in her revision of the poem's opening lines:

> Leaving home
> when I was seventeen,
> I remembered ten years before,
> when Dad married you;
> you were a child, still,
> at thirty-three.
> If only I had been as wise back then
> as I was at seventeen—

Having now made it apparent that "Seventeen" is addressed to the speaker's "step-Mom," Charity has also made the situation, its time frame, and the consequently difficult relationship between step-mother, father, and daughter accessible and understandable. The finished poem is thus at once a letter to her step-mother, to her larger audience of readers/eavesdroppers, and to her critiquing correspondents in the class.

Asking student writers to try their hand at letter poems benefits their growth as poets in various ways. It requires them both to define a rhetorical audience—which gives their work purposeful focus while stimulating an honest confrontation with their own experience—and to consider a real audience, which leads to the development of effective poetic techniques for sharing that experience concretely. Finally, in sending their drafts out to their fellow writers for response and revising accordingly, the students have concluded a multi-layered dialogue that can culminate in poems as strong as the following:

> Evidence of My Life
> *For Craig*
>
> I am afraid to write
> something you might see,
> hand you
>
> the evidence of my life,
> tempt you into the
> biography beyond
>
> the poem, or worse,
> offend you when I
> suppose the future,

crafting intimacy
out of citrus and
fire, and flower and

crossing bridges,
splitting apples,
coring them and

then each other;
supposing us is
dangerous,

sweetheart, but
proscribing us,
evading tomorrows,

this is not romance.

I carry cognizance
into the bedroom
where I

pronounce myself
in simple
rhythms, and you

read the what
and not the why
of me, whereby

I am not to be
questioned,
whereby

I am not to be
written,
and you are happy.

                    Laurie

Letter poems are not an easy undertaking for many students who are un-
used to, or fearful of, handing others the "evidence" of their lives, "pronounc-
ing" themselves, as Laurie has done so effectively here. It is not easy to open
up, and own up to, one's failures, dissatisfactions, uncertainties, or even one's
boundless joys, to someone else, as writing poems asks one to do. But to begin
a poem with the intention of real communication with another—to acknowledge, yes, "this is just to say" something I need to tell you whether you can hear
it or not—is to begin to write the kind of poem that Emily Dickinson called a
"letter to the world."

Notes

1. My thanks to my students in English 119, Advanced Poetry Writing, Spring 1997, for permission to use their poems, critiques, and questionnaire responses in this chapter.

2. Some of the letter poems to be found in *Contemporary American Poetry* include "To Dorothy," Marvin Bell; "Poem for James Wright," Robert Bly; "the mother," Gwendolyn Brooks; "Letter from Slough Pond," Isabella Gardner; "Love Poem," Louise Gluck; "Letter," Robert Hass; from *The Blessing,* Carolyn Kizer ; "How It Is," Maxine Kumin; "The City In Which I Love You," Li-Young Lee; "Ways of Conquest," Denise Levertov; "To My Dead Father," Frank O'Hara; "You Ask Why Sometimes I Say Stop," Marge Piercy; "With Mercy for the Greedy," Anne Sexton; "The Big War," Charles Simic; and "Letter to Jean-Paul Baudot, at Christmas," Lucien Stryk.

4

"Letters from Beyond"

Reading Dante as a Writer

William Stephany

Dante can be daunting. He makes casual reference in his work to an enormous range of material—from political history, literary history, and church history; from medieval poetry, classical literature, and mythology; from philosophy, theology, and the Bible; from his own biography—so many references that in most translations, the explanatory notes are longer than the text itself. For most readers, this means that the *Divine Comedy* needs to be studied in order to be read. For me, this means that I need to do more "explaining" in the Dante course than in any of my others. And the effect is that first-time readers can sometimes feel swamped by the experience and cling to my explanations just to stay afloat, threatening to make the class a passive experience. Students sometimes learn to admire the poem, rather than enjoy it or internalize it as part of their own intellectual and cultural heritage.

To try to combat this problem in the Spring 1998 semester, instead of more traditional academic assignments, I asked my thirty students (sophomore-to-senior English majors) to write, as the only writing in the course, twelve letters, four each on *Inferno, Purgatorio,* and *Paradiso.* The fourth letter on each canticle—Letters four, eight, and twelve—was to be longer, was to be written to me, and was to provide a summary retrospective response to the entire canticle we were completing. Only these three longer fourth letters were given a grade, with the earlier letters serving as exploratory drafts. The syllabus introduced the assignment, in part, as follows:

```
The structure of Dante's poem is loosely that of
travel writing, with Dante telling his readers about
a journey that he claims to have completed through
hell, purgatory, and heaven. The "real" foreign coun-
try for most twentieth-century American students,
```

however, is not so much the fictional Otherworld through which he claims to travel as Dante's world itself, whose values, cultural vocabulary, and pre-suppositions can be unsettling and alienating in ways akin to foreign travel. And most of you will be spending 20% of your academic time this semester in Dante World! One of the classic ways in which people make sense of foreign travel is by extensive letter writing, usually to family and friends back home, writing which keeps loved ones informed of your ac-tivities, but which just as importantly requires you to articulate for yourself your responses to the strange new world you are discovering. Letters of that sort are written for your own benefit as much as for the benefit of your correspondent — *more* for your own benefit, usually, since they are often responses that you would not otherwise remember.[1]

At first, I asked students to address these letters typically to a friend or family member, but suggested that they could also write a letter to me, to classmates, to Dante, or to a character Dante meets in the poem. Alternatively, they could write a letter in the voice of one of the characters in the poem to someone else. For several reasons, as I'll discuss below, once past *Inferno,* I asked them typ-ically to write to me.

The letters students wrote on (or from) hell covered a wide range. In addi-tion to letters to family or friends about their experiences, others included: a letter from Dante to Freud, one from Beatrice to Virgil, another from Virgil to Beatrice, a summary of a group tour of hell, hints to future travelers with a list of supplies to be sure to pack, and (from the first *Purgatorio* letter) an entry from Dante's diary with a "To-Do List" detailing all the tasks he'd promised souls he'd undertake on their behalf once back in Italy. Another student wrote a series of four letters from *Inferno* to friends back home (really a fairly sub-stantial narrative of some fifteen single-spaced pages by the time he finished with it) about suffering a bike accident in Italy and then regaining conscious-ness on a straw pallet in a stuccoed room where he's being nursed by Beatrice who reads letters from Dante—sort of "The Italian Patient."

It's difficult for me to quote from, rather than paraphrase, such letters as these. They don't lend themselves to excerpting, in part because of the letter format itself. Letter writers assume a shared history with correspondents, and details necessary to their comprehension are typically suppressed in letters where both the writer and recipient (and, in this case, the "real" intended audi-ence—I and others in the class) have experiences in common: here a body of knowledge about the poem, its textual commentary, and our class discussions. However, there's no way to convey the spirit of a course such as this without direct quotation, since the proof of the process is in the letters' details. Most of the following examples, therefore, will be "stand-alone" portions of letters—excerpts whose rhetorical effect does not require specific knowledge of the poem. In citing examples, I'll provide the number of the letter as well as the student's name, since the letter's number identifies the time of semester as well as the point reached in the poem. Letter two, for example, was the second on *Inferno* and came, therefore, roughly $\frac{2}{12}$ of the way—$\frac{1}{6}$ of the way—into the semester.

Some of the letters did a good job of "defamiliarizing" the poem (to borrow a term from Russian Formalist criticism), restoring the strangeness of a text that's too easily reduced to the commonplace by its notes. In her second letter, written from hell to her older brother Pat, Sharon wrote:

```
Ah, yes, the crowds. One member of our tour group, a
guy named Dante, has been annoying me a bit. He and
the spirit known as Virgil seem to be on a mission
of some sort (I get the impression that Dante is writ-
ing a story about this place), so the only members of
the aforementioned crowds that we get to talk to are
the ones Dante knows, and many of them are people he
knows personally. Fortunately, I've heard of some of
them, but it's getting difficult to keep all of the
names straight in my mind; there's a sort of direc-
tory that we all had to purchase, before boarding the
busses that got us here, but I find myself having to
consult it quite frequently.
```

Jason writes home to his Mom in his third letter: "I'm going to give you some more information on this Dante character, whom I mentioned before. Since my last letter I have found out that he's planning to write a tell-all book about Hell, sort of an *Inferno* exposé." Amanda wrote her third letter to God, identifying herself at the end with her signature and the words "Created: 1-17-76 (remember?)."

My Responses

After each of the first three sets of letters, I responded by letter to the class as a group. In each letter, I confined myself to two single-spaced pages. They gave me an opportunity to praise (and provide models of) good student writing, to model a level of discourse for student letters, to try to nudge subsequent letters toward more serious commitments, and to respond to specific student questions, introducing early in the semester concepts that might otherwise go unexpressed. In my first letter, for example, I dealt with details of format and housekeeping raised in student letters, praised specific student writing, offered advice about how to write more effectively in future letters, and addressed a commonly asked question about the placement of the virtuous pagans in Limbo. Several students were troubled that, despite their accomplishments and moral probity, these people were consigned to hell (even if to hell's most attractive alcove), and they were troubled that these souls no longer had an opportunity to better their situation: this is where they would be forever. What kind of a God would do such a thing, several students wanted to know. In responding, I tried to shift attention from the justice of their placement in Limbo (a question I wanted to leave open as we proceeded through the poem), and addressed the question of the poem's central representational premise. In Charles S. Singleton's now axiomatic phrase, "the fiction of this poem is that it's not fiction," and it was extremely helpful to be able to introduce this concept so early in the poem and in response to student confusion over this very issue: they had taken the placement of souls as evidence of God's judgment, not of Dante's.

In my other two letters, I again cited specific examples of good student writing, made suggestions about how to read Dante effectively, and responded to some specific questions in ways designed to introduce some medieval modes of thinking early in the semester. For example, I addressed a commonly expressed surprise over Dante's treatment of homosexuals by discussing the survival into the Middle Ages of Aristotelian notions of final causality. In response to observations about how "hard" Dante is, how much he expects his readers to know, I asked students to imagine themselves in the fourteenth century, when the handmade book was the high point in the technology of information transmission and retrieval, when the Protestant Reformation, seemingly "inevitable" to us in retrospect, would have been an unimaginable prospect, when writing "serious" literature founded on classical learning and doing so in a language other than Latin would have been a daring choice.

I stopped writing these responses after the first three letters, frankly because of lack of time. Since Letters 4 and following were usually addressed to me (as explained below) and since they often asked (or sometimes implied) specific *ad hoc* questions, I found that I did not have time for both individual responses and general collective letters. Instead, I wrote short notes back to students at the end of their letters, addressing issues they had raised (in addition to responding marginally as appropriate). The choice to shift to specific responses seems to have been a good one: in evaluating the course, several students commented on the importance of this ongoing dialogue with me.

My responses did more than just address specific questions about content, especially for students who seemed insecure about their ability to handle such a demanding text. A couple of the students were simultaneously enrolled in a Latin class where they were reading some of Dante's sources in the original language, and a few others were taking Bible as Literature. But for most, the range of Dante's references was an experience in cultural immersion. In my responses to every student letter during the semester, therefore, I tried to find something specific to praise: I looked for opportunities to catch students in the act of being smart, on the assumption that students acting in good faith would live up to my expectations of them. I tried to act as a cheerleader, especially for students who doubted their abilities and needed reassurance. I recalled hearing Donald Murray once suggest that the best model for a writing teacher might be an athletic coach. This approach also had an interesting effect on me as a reader of student papers. With traditional grading, too often I read through student papers marking errors; here I found myself reading student letters marking insights. When students did make mistakes in reading the poem or betrayed their ignorance of cultural history or of literary convention, I responded as a letter writer, without tying the response to a grade: with the focus on communication rather than evaluation, students seemed to exhale and allow themselves the fun of learning the poem. As a result, students became better readers of Dante, even as his poem became more difficult and therefore demanded better readers.

Mid-Course Correction

For many students the original assignment prompted inspired writing; in truth, however, the "creative response" letters on *Inferno* were not always successful. Some letters became so preoccupied with persona or voice or setting that they dealt with Dante's text in cavalier fashion, if at all. If the creative problems had always been cleverly solved, this might be no great problem, but these letters were sometimes formulaic, letters to family and friends too often lacked an edge, and some letters seemed written in haste and without sufficient reflection. After our third letter, some students engaged in a virtual discussion on our course e-mail list, expressing their anxiety about feeling required to deal with the material as a traveler, rather than as a reader. I had already announced that letter four, the first of the longer letters, was to be written to me, and when it produced a larger percentage of engaged and intelligent responses to the poem, I asked students to consider this format the norm for the rest of the semester, leaving open the possibility of more experimental letters where this seemed appropriate, but making them now the less-common format. My original attempt to invite creative responses had been read as a command performance, and students seemed relieved to learn that they did not have to fabricate a voice each week (though they did do so on occasion) when a straightforward letter to me might serve them better. As a result, those letters later in the semester that *were* creative were more likely to be successful.

As the semester moved from *Inferno* to *Purgatorio* I felt some of my usual anxiety: hell is more immediately attractive to modern readers than Purgatory or Paradise, and students' focus can sometimes waver as the semester progresses.[2] But the letters seemed to help them stay on track: in their end-of-semester evaluations of the letters, students frequently claimed that the letters helped them keep up on the reading. More than this, they welcomed the way the openness of letters empowered them to make discoveries they might otherwise have missed. For my part, I was impressed by the range of writing that the assignment seems to have made possible, from analytical, to speculative, to personal, to reflective, to theoretical.

Some letters were *analytical,* as in this paragraph from John C.'s fifth letter:

> Dante reminds me to a certain extent of the Roman poet Horace. Horace also lamented the bitter civil wars and in-fighting that were plaguing Rome. This at a time when the late Republic was in its death throes and empire on the way. Towards the end of his poems, however, the civil wars were becoming largely a memory. Horace earnestly prayed that Augustus Caesar was the answer to those troubled times and the bringer of peace. Dante hopes for many of the same things in his Comedy. He sees Italy destroying itself again, and like Horace before him, Dante sees peace in the empire. However, [for Dante] this time the empire will have the blessing and support of God through the Catholic church.

John was a Latin minor, and this passage serves also to show how students were able to bring to their letters what they had learned elsewhere. Others with specialized backgrounds wrote about Dante and science and Dante and math. A business minor applied various economic theories to analyze Dante's attitudes about money. Those of us who teach Dante regularly assert that his text is inherently interdisciplinary; this assignment allowed some students to make this discovery for themselves.

Some letters were *speculative,* as in this passage from Sharon's final letter:

> . . . as Dante shows, it is intellectual and spiritual development that enables one to keep an excessive desire for material goods in check. Such desires grow up to fill the voids left by a lack of intellectual and spiritual development or fulfillment, in my opinion. I wonder what Dante would make of the consumerist economy and culture of our modern-day United States? I wonder what he would think about the ways in which U.S. culture is affecting the rest of the world?

Some letters were *personal,* as in this from Peter's eighth letter (the Statius he refers to is a character from *Purgatorio*):

> Just as Statius misread, to the benefit of his salvation, Virgil's *Aeneid,* so will I now attempt to read parallels between Dante's *Purgatorio* and my own

> Alternative Spring Break experience of two weeks
> ago. . . . I'll do as Statius did, which is to make
> a poem do what I need it to do, regardless of its
> original purpose . . . and use it for my own spiri-
> tual advantage, which is the only way I can make it
> through any written test right now after having
> learned more in a week outside of school than in a
> good long time in it.

As in this case, the letter assignment often provided reminders that school is only part of our students' lives. From a narrow point of view, a letter of this sort might seem "off-topic," but as a learning tool, it may have been essential in helping Peter acknowledge the static in his life, so he could tune it out and improve his reception of Dante.

Letters could be *reflective,* as with Jill's fifth letter on the way souls in Purgatory—as opposed to those in Hell—react to finding a living person among them:

> This reaction seems to imply that the souls possess
> curiosity. The confusion matters to them, they don't
> just accept that he is living and shrug it off, they
> want to know more, they are mystified. This wanting to
> know reminds me of the typical traits of a good stu-
> dent, one who is puzzled and who asks questions.

And letters could be *theoretical,* as in this excerpt from Sharon's final letter:

> But what's so wonderful about reading this poem is
> that it is such a shining example of how science and
> philosophy can come together in art to inform ideol-
> ogy or world-view — and how that ideology gets re-
> flected back into science and philosophy. It's the in-
> verted diorama of the universe as seen in the Primum
> Mobile of Cantos XXVIII and XXIX all over again — God
> envisioned as containing and contained by all. Did
> Dante invent chaos mathematics — the theory of reiter-
> ation in which each part reflects the whole? In a very
> convoluted way, maybe he did, through the effect his
> poem has had on Western culture. I don't think it's
> any accident that Dante's vision reminds me of unified
> field theory, or that some of his insights seem to
> foreshadow current philosophical and scientific de-
> velopments — nor do I think it's evidence that Dante
> was in fact a prophet invested by God with certain
> knowledge of future events. Rather, it's evidence for

how our ways of thinking and doing things, including
our methods of scientific inquiry, reflect the history
of our culture. Cultural values get preserved – or
maybe "preserved" isn't the right word, because cultural values don't stay the same, and in fact they
sometimes get twisted into new and dangerous things,
but they do tend to "reiterate" – and the seemingly
miraculous relevance of Dante to the modern world is
an example of that. His way of seeing the world, even
while it modifies, revolutionizes, distorts to his
own meaning, nevertheless also reflects the ideology
of his day.

The writing captures the tentativeness of language in the act of thinking: "Cultural values get preserved—or maybe 'preserved' isn't the right word." But it
also explores complex issues about scientific language as an expression of a
culture, about the way literature produces and reproduces cultural forms even
as it imitates them, about the way the present is embedded in the past. The letter format—informal, yet slightly elevated in tone, combined with an ongoing
awareness of "another" to whom you must be clear—may make it better suited
than, for example, the journal as a vehicle for this kind of speculation.

Summary Letters

The three longer summary letters—numbers four, eight, and twelve—seemed
to have been an effective tool with which students could look back through the
text, through the semester, through their own previous writing and thinking, re-
viewing former ideas to draw new conclusions. In a sense, it helped restore the
etymological sense to the word "revision." In Letter eight, Kurt wrote: I have
found the final letter of each book to be the most rewarding because it has
allowed me to retrospectively look at the books. This has allowed for new avenues of travel and for travel down old avenues, but with different perspectives
from the original thought process." And John P. wrote in his eighth letter:

Looking back, I have much more of a sense of Hell's
being self-contained, in a way. In fact, I am now much
more aware of the fact that Hell was about contain-
ment, entrapment, confinement, imprisonment, etc. Upon
completing *Inferno*, after having so easily broken
free from its bounds, I understood on one level that
this was what Hell was about, but as a reader I
didn't feel the powerful grab. . . . My first impres-
sion, after finishing *Purgatorio*, was that of confusion. It started to dawn on me though, for the first

```
time really, that this confusion — something that had
troubled me throughout the ascent — was a function of
profound freedom.
```

The retrospective letters also allowed students to explore earlier questions with
the advantage of additional knowledge of the poem. One of the unusual conventions Dante devises for *Paradiso* is that souls in heaven can read Dante's
mind and answer his questions before he formulates them. This troubled Kate
in Letters 9–11 and she never did reconcile herself to the premise, but in Letter twelve she was able to articulate for herself the special demands that the
process places on us as readers:

```
As I look back on my earlier letters, I note that I
had difficulty with the long speeches. I found it hard
to follow what each soul was telling Dante and even
more difficult because the souls could read Dante's
mind and therefore a question was never posed. That
annoying behavior made it extremely difficult because
many times I would have to figure out what the ques-
tion was just by the answer, somewhat like playing
Jeopardy!
```

It *is,* in fact, difficult to understand passages of this sort—rather like overhear-
ing half of a telephone conversation—and the chance to return and reconsider
the episodes in her final letter allowed Kate the opportunity to identify the
rhetorical process for herself.

Evaluations

On the final day of the semester, I asked students to write in response to the following prompt:

```
Evaluate  the  Letter  experiment.  What  were  its
strengths for you? Its weaknesses? Did it help you in
"learning the poem"? In keeping up with and reacting
to Dante's intellectual and artistic concerns?
```

I was impressed by the thoughtfulness of the students' responses: the course
seems to have inspired them to reflection, and if the evaluations provided feedback about the course, they also were themselves often examples of good writing. Most students were extremely positive. Two students said that journals
would have served them as well as letters did and perhaps less "artificially,"
while at the opposite extreme two students lamented the lost opportunity to
write formal academic papers on Dante. This served as a reminder that there
are students who feel comfortable with the forms of traditional academic writing and who welcome the particular opportunity they provide to pursue complicated problems in depth and in breadth and with precision. One of these stu-

dents, in fact, solved the problem for herself by writing analytical papers within the letter format. "Dear Prof. Stephany," she would begin, and she would conclude with "Sincerely," followed by a signature, but everything in between would be a formal paper about the week's reading.[3]

The vast majority of the class endorsed the letter format enthusiastically. Several remarked on the way the letters helped establish a supportive learning environment while dealing with a complex and challenging subject. One begins: "I think the greatest value of the letter-writing experiment derived from the informality. In such a reduced-stress situation, it was possible to discover the process of connection with a text." Another begins: "The letter experiment at first seemed a little too 'easy.' But as the weeks rolled by, its 'easiness' translated into a desirable freedom. . . . The letter assignment became an arena to either expand on class discussion or to adventure into new territories. The structural element also proved a strength, especially for me as a quite easily disenfranchised individual. I would choose letters over papers, not because it appears easier but because it offers us so much room."

Several students wrote that the letters made them better readers. One claimed: "The letters helped me to grasp the difficult ideas in Dante because I had to articulate and explain what I was struggling with. The letters were also, I think, a great way to provide individual growth. I don't know about other people, but I can definitely see how I became more comfortable with the material in the poem, and I began to attack the harder concepts." One commented that to write the letters, "You have to read so carefully, and at the same time you end up having to read the material *SO* many times." Another said that the letters "made me think more and analyze sections of the poem I might otherwise have overlooked," and yet another said, "the letters every week really forced me to stay on top of things—not just for retention of specifics, but to promote and foster thoughtful, analytical critiques of the reading we did each week."

Conclusions

Ultimately, the best evidence that the assignment had worked may be the number of final letters and course evaluations that lamented the end of the course: the assignment seemed to have kept the students engaged and committed to the end. Jason began his final letter (playing with a figure of speech from Canto 2 of *Paradiso*):

> Here we are, finally, at the end. Somehow I've managed
> to keep my little boat afloat, though I was taking on
> water for a while. And while I think Dante would be
> a little disappointed in my very basic understanding
> of the poem, I'm proud that I managed to get through
> it and managed to have a pretty good idea as to what
> was going on. That's enough patting myself on the

```
back, I've still got to tell you about the last twelve
cantos.
```

And Sharon concluded her final letter:

```
. . . I'm reluctant to write the last lines. I don't
want the course to end — just like I didn't want to
say good-bye to Virgil, just like I wanted one more
scene at the end of Paradiso. But — time presses on-
ward, and it reminds me unmercifully that I have so
many other things to do this week.⁴
```

One last excerpt from a Letter twelve. The closer Dante got to the end of the poem, the more he resorted to what medieval rhetoric called the *ineffability topos,* the claim (in words, of course) that the experience of being outside of time and space cannot be expressed in words. John P. devised his own version of an *ineffability topos* in his final letter:

```
This is that bittersweet moment of the journey where
my sadness at leaving such an exotic voyage is coun-
termanded by my desire to get my weary bones home for
rest. But WOW, what a sendoff! I mean, I'm gonna
hafta book those travel agents again. Let me try to
describe what I sa... That is, let me explain the
feast that lay before my unfettered imagin . . . What
I'm trying to say is . . . Well, suffice it to say
that whoever, or whatever it was that my guide and I
came upon was so utterly indescribable that I'm left
with an exasperated collection of unfinished sen-
tences. I'm not sure how, but the experience was that
of plenitude, culmination, fruition, climax. . . .
There, it happened again! Every time I try to imag-
ine the situation, not only my words, but my thoughts
and feelings fall short of the capability to express
the inexpressible. This feeling of ineptitude is the
biggest clue I have that the trip would seem to be
over. I can only say that I never felt before, nor will
ever feel again, the profound sense of freedom that
pervaded the strange place (non-place, really) in
which I found myself eternally present. The one thing
that I fail to understand is how I got back here, how
I find myself once again glued into the confines of
spatio-temporal locale.
```

I didn't know what to expect when I made this assignment; I've been teach-ing the poem for thirty years, but never with letters. What I found is that this format led many students to read the *Comedy* as writers. As one student evaluation put it: "If nothing else, knowing that I had to write a letter made me read the poem a little better because I was *looking* for something to write about that'd be fun, scouring the text for something to write about." Another wrote: "I found myself picking apart each Canto, searching for something to base my letter upon." A third wrote: "I often think best in writing, and remember best what I have written down. The letters helped me grapple with Dante's ideas, and they gave me a 'safe' place in which to do so—not to mention a *forum* in which to do so *fully*, more fully that I would have been able to through class participation alone." Another wrote that "'normal' papers force students to draw conclusions *before* they write, whereas the letters allowed us to write *through* the process." And yet another claimed that the letters "held my interest better, which is a positive because writing about this poem was the best way for me to analyze it and since I enjoyed the writing, I enjoyed the poem better."

Sharon was one of the most articulate writers in the class, and I'll return to her as I conclude. As I suggested at the beginning of this chapter, I was concerned that Dante's poem too often feels like a "masterpiece" to students, something whose demands and whose cultural eminence place it outside of their experience. But the letters seemed to have brought the text back into human scale for them. In her fifth letter, in describing the radical difference she had found between the imagery of *Purgatorio* and that of *Inferno,* Sharon listed and summarized four images that struck her as "particularly beautiful," and added: "Ok—that's probably enough about images; my point is that the writing isn't so 'hellbound' anymore! (Can you imagine . . . critiquing the Comedy in a writing workshop?)" She catches herself, parenthetically, in the act of having treated Dante as "just another writer," in fact, catches herself in the act of having applied to the *Comedy* techniques she had learned to apply to the work of other students in a writing seminar.[5]

One final observation: the letter experiment also encouraged me to teach differently—in degree, if not in kind. In my *ad hoc* responses to student letters, I was always aware of the individual I was writing to, especially as I came to know the students, their interests, and their familiarity with the spirit and forms of traditional European culture. Meanwhile, in the early-semester letters to the class as a whole, I was always aware of audience and tone and my rhetorical objectives. Student letters helped me to understand some specific needs to be addressed, and I was able to intervene in a timely fashion—typically only a week "late." And since it was usually not material I had previously taught in a Dante class, at least not in this way, I was required to do so in careful language selected for this particular occasion. I found that I was always aware that I was teaching students as well as the course's subject matter, and while we all try to do this all the time, Dante is the kind of complex subject that can distract a teacher—and maybe especially an experienced teacher—from this awareness. In short, the letters may have encouraged me, too, to approach the course more as a writer.

Notes

1. In part, I came up with this way of conceiving the assignment because I had just read Kenneth Wagner and Tony Magistrale's *Writing Across Culture: An Introduction to Study Abroad and the Writing Process* (Lang 1995).

2. When Johanna, in her fifth letter, wrote, "I must tell you that the further we get from Hell, the better I like this poem," it was music to a Dante teacher's ears: many of "us" come to prefer Purgatory and Paradise, but for students this often seems to be an acquired taste.

3. Three other students who loved the letter format noted "that they would have led naturally into writing a formal paper," while also acknowledging that it would have been difficult to find the time for this in the course. I had decided from the outset that the best way to valorize the letters and conduct the course's pedagogical experiment was to use only letters in the course. Perhaps in the future I'd try for some balance with other forms of writing.

4. Virgil disappears from the poem quite suddenly and stunningly in *Purgatorio* 30, a moment which retains its power to shock readers. Another student in her final letter made the identical observation in passing: "Is it over already? Reading the last cantos of *Paradiso* was worse than saying good-bye to Virgil at the end of *Purgatorio*."

5. This was the kind of class which Ghita Orth writes about in Chapter 3 in this book.

5

Teaching the Epistolary Novel Through E-mail

Philip Baruth

To the undergraduates in my eighteenth-century English literature courses, everything—every textual production from every genre—is a novel. When we read autobiography, they tell me, "This novel didn't really do it for me"; when we read philosophy, say Edmund Burke's *Philosophical Enquiry,* they'll report that "Burke's novel" took a lot more time and outlining than they'd anticipated.

It's not that they don't understand the difference between a novel and an autobiography. They do: they realize that one is fiction, and the other a highly subjective self-history. It's just that the word "novel" seems to have opened up and flattened out for them, to the point where it describes any lengthy prose production, but especially those that they encounter in English classes. A book, even if otherwise indicated, is a novel.

Nothing could more clearly demonstrate the way in which the novel, having come to prominence in the eighteenth century, has reshaped the Western literary universe in the ensuing two centuries. And, by extension, nothing could more clearly demonstrate the continuing need for students to understand the genesis and history of the novel.

The problem is (and has been for several academic generations) that students generally don't like eighteenth-century novels. There are notable exceptions, but on the whole, I think it's fair to say that given a choice between *Moll Flanders* and *Oliver Twist,* between Tobias Smollett and Louisa May Alcott, students will gratefully choose the *Twist* and Alcott. And the eighteenth-century novel that they despise more than any other—and I report this as one who loves the sub-genre myself—is the epistolary novel, the story told in letters. Given a choice, no contemporary freshman will ever, ever choose *Pamela,* to say nothing of Richardson's follow-up *Clarissa,* which at 1600 pages was not only twice as long but twice as big a hit with the eighteenth-century reading public. While the basic epistolary plots (most, like Richardson's, a variation on the sexual seduction of or threat to a virginal young woman) seem familiar enough from

Hollywood thrillers and horror films, the means of prose exposition inevitably puts students to sleep.

At least this *was* my experience, until about five or six year ago, when I began to notice that something was changing. Students seemed less resistent to epistolary novels like Fanny Burney's *Evelina,* the story of a young woman entering the highest levels of London society and writing home to her foster-father about the trials associated with it. Class discussion was less perfunctory, more engaged. The students seemed to be having less difficulty imagining the complex interweaving of correspondence at the heart of the form. And they began in fits and starts to relate the epistolary novel's narrative features to their own experience with electronic mail.

E-mail and Epistolary Narrative

For a telephonic culture, one given to communicating verbally, promiscuously and haphazardly, it is difficult to imagine the highly deliberate letter-writing culture of Britain in the early modern period. Richardson's "writing to the moment"—his technique of having present-tense action break into the actual writing of the letter—had always struck my students (and me, in certain moments) as unbearably stagey. Who would continue writing, as Pamela does, during the very moments when her would-be seducer is pounding on the door? How could letter writing possibly have been so indivisible from lived events for people of Richardson's period? Finally, how could we accept the sheer volume of correspondence theoretically represented by a 1600-page novel like *Clarissa?* Who could care for that long, about anything? These were questions I had always been able to answer only very imperfectly.

But then, in a spurt of technological evolution, e-mail answered them for me. Suddenly my students understood, because in the span of a very small number of years electronic letter writing became crucial to their daily lives as well. I've informally polled my classes and found that on the average they check their e-mail accounts twice or three times a day. Again, that is the average; some admitted to addiction, to checking ten or twelve times a day, while a nonchalant few make correspondence an every-other-day affair. But for the majority, e-mail is something they do upon waking; during the lunch hour; by way of making plans for the evening; and in late-night moments of composition that rival Evelina's, electronic jags that sometimes go on for hours.

In other words, students have very quickly learned to interweave their living and their letter writing to the point where they are all but inseparable. They no longer have problems imagining Pamela's desire to write to the last possible instant; their own e-mail style tends toward the same stylized reluctance to leave off. As students reported in class discussion, they characteristically write to the last moment, and often make a point of stressing this brinksmanship to their correspondent by explaining why they must stop. They do so, I think, to stress their devotion, in much the same way Pamela and Evelina continually re-assure their parents/guardians. If life would allow, they seem to say, I'd stay connected always.

In this way, e-mail has given students a pure, fresh, intuitive grasp of epis-tolary form. The maze-like correspondence that makes up Richardson's *Clarissa* is in fact more easily understood, more easily digested, than their own e-mail correspondences, which include ongoing narratives with friends, e-mail circu-lars forwarded by all-but-anonymous individuals somewhere else in cyber-space, group posts, etc. The person-to-person letter is at the cell-level of elec-tronic web technology; students now effortlessly intuit not only the cell itself but the body of correspondence called into being by billions of individuals worldwide.

While I was grateful for this new broad-based intuition, I felt that if students could bring the connections between these forms to consciousness by creating fictional correspondences themselves, they would establish a more lasting and meaningful connection to what is arguably the earliest novelistic form. And so after assigning them Burney's *Evelina,* I set them the task of creating their own epistolary narrative, but one framed in the form of electronic messages. Though the form of letter differed, I urged them to take Clarissa's words as their cue: "I have deposited my narrative down to this day noon; but I hope soon to follow it with another letter, that I may keep you as little a while as possible in that suspense, which I am so much affected by at this moment" (256).

The Electronic Epistle: Shaping the Updated Narrative

Fanny Burney's *Evelina,* a quirky and funny novel, formed the basis for this as-signment. Unlike Richardson's epistolary epics—which typically come in at well over 1,000 pages, complete with didactic postscripts and lists of *dramatis personae*—Burney's novel is a manageable classroom text at under 500 pages. More importantly, Burney's often surprisingly biting satire serves to offset the heavy moralizing that continued to characterize the form throughout the cen-tury. Some scenes, such as one in which two drunken young aristocrats race eighty-year-old women across a gravel course for money, never fail to shock students into discussion.

As we neared the end of Burney's text—and our discussion of the simi-larities between e-mail and eighteenth-century letter-writing culture—I asked students to begin making notes for a fiction of their own. I wanted them to pro-duce a short fictional correspondence, this consisting of any number of indi-vidual e-mail messages between two primary correspondents, although I did not limit them to two. They were free either to work with another student, and thus use *actual* e-mail to construct the correspondence, or to use their individ-ual word processors to mimic the look of an e-mail exchange. Below is the as-signment sheet I passed out to them:

Writing The E-mail "Novel"
English 85: Texts and Contexts

As we've talked about in class this week, the eighteenth-century epistolary novel took a popular existing "technology" — the personal letter — and built it into a highly complex, cumulative narrative form. Richardson's novels came to run well over fifteen hundred pages by the end of his career, but his audiences quite literally cried when they'd finished them, both because they tended to be tragedies and because there was no more to read.

I'd like you to attempt the same thing, by taking a popular current technology — the e-mail letter — and finding ways to build it into an ongoing story, with twists and turns and unexpected outcomes, suspense in a word.

The Method:

There are two main ways to create this e-mail narrative: by yourself, or with a partner. If you work by yourself, you will use your normal word-processing software to mimic e-mail format (writing time and date and sender name at the top, etc.) as best you can. In this case, you would never use real e-mail at all, but simply create an authentic facsimile. Verisimilitude — a cleverly made illusion of reality — will make or break your work. The other method involves working with a partner, sending him or her the first letter, to which they reply, making sure to keep the story moving and building. If you work with a partner, it would be best to plan out the overall shape and themes and incidents of the correspondence *before* you begin trading the actual component messages. Suppose your partner sends you a "letter" in which her new male neighbor seems charming, helpful and polite. In keeping with the traditional foreshadowing pattern from Burney and Richardson, you might send back a message counseling her to be on her guard with him. Two messages later, she reports that he's gone over the line from being helpful to something of an annoyance, even a little overbearing or strange — and your story is off and running.

Some Things to Remember:

You'll need to look much more carefully than we did in class at how these novelists *begin* their stories. Since the reader is looking over the shoulder of the fictional writers, authors can't simply give a summary of the action. They have to drop enough explanatory hints in the course of normal correspondence to bring the reader into the action. Similarly, you'll need to look at the various techniques used to build suspense, such as having a character "write to the moment," that is, write even as suspenseful action is occurring. Under what circumstances could you imagine being at a computer typing while action occurred near or around you? Hollywood has been using this technique for years; think of cyberthrillers like *Sneakers, The Net,* etc.

Remember also these tricks we discussed in class, and think how you might adapt them to e-mail:

- Characters forge letters to one another, fooling the reader as well, and then reveal the forgery several letters later.
- Characters insert poetry, devotional prose, etc., into their letters, broadening the kinds of allusions and effects they can achieve.
- Writing "in continuation." Richardson and Burney realized that constant back-and-forth could be annoying, so often they would have a character compile a kind of letter diary which could then be sent in a packet to the reader. This allowed for longer scene construction, or even a sequence of scenes, without distracting the reader of the novel.
- Sometimes letters get read by people other than those they were intended to reach.

E-mail has a "globalizing" function (which you use to "cc" someone) that often mistakenly results in messages going out to a whole network of readers. Can you design this in?

Format: Five pages if working alone, ten if working as a team. Final product should look like an e-mail "thread," messages chained to one another as responses. Treat the finished product with every bit as

```
much technical care as you would a critical essay;
they must be grammatically clean, carefully proof-
read, and cunningly outlined prior to writing.
```

Their responses were fascinating, both for ways in which they worked and ways in which they didn't. The submissions tended to fall into three broad categories: those who simply turned in seemingly random e-mail, those who flirted with plot but were ultimately unable to keep one up and running, and those who took naturally to the form.

The small but unavoidable percentage of students in the first category turned in correspondences that no doubt mirrored those they engage in every day: fairly random exchanges with no organizing plot or tension, in which each writer discusses a number of unconnected events in his or her life. These "fictions" read more like casual small talk than anything novelistic. Coming as they did on the heels of explicit discussion about constructing plot, these particular responses led me to believe that e-mail has its own very powerful ethic of randomness—clearly some students couldn't or wouldn't view it as a directed, scripted format. To do so, they seemed tacitly to be saying, would be to bring rules to a world they prefer to see as rule-free.

The second group, those who came close to putting together a plot, seemed to understand the assignment but were somehow unable to put it completely into practice. A good example is an exchange between "Howie" and "Teresa," a recently engaged couple separated for the Christmas holidays. At first it seems that the engagement has been a secret, and that the revelation of the truth will power the narrative. But this plotline proves a red herring—Howie remarks in his third letter that he has "told everyone," to which his fiance responds, "I'm just excited that we have told everyone about the engagement and it's out in the open." Thus ends the secret-marriage threat.

Similarly, Howie writes in several letters about slightly escalating conflicts with his father. At one point, he complains to Teresa that he separated all the gifts under the Christmas tree according to recipient, "but Dad got all pissed off and yelled at me. He told me to put them all back the way they were." The small scene ends with Howie recreating a mini-lecture from his father on the real religious reason for the Christmas holiday. This letter is followed immediately by another in which Howie's father plays Pavarotti incessantly, and lectures him on the music. "I think Dad has played it about ten times today already. . . . I guess that's something you'll have to put up with about my family . . . we are repetitive :)"

Yet, this letter marks the end of any mention of the father, and a set of clearly emerging plotlines—in which the father provides unexpectedly valuable advice for the young prospective groom, say, or in which the young man has to break away from overbearing paternal authority—fades from sight. As I suggested before, the students in this category seem to understand the assignment; they realize that they need to stick with certain subject matter, to create a continuity of theme. And they were able to tell me verbally, in office hours, their plans for the assignment. But somewhere along the way the proposed plots failed to materialize fully.

But the final and largest number of students turned out fictions which more than exceeded my expectations. Evelina's sometimes breathless letters—which are actually much more composed than Pamela's or Clarissa's—they matched with their own profusion of exclamation points and emphasis marks and pictographic "emoticons": "It's Christmas Eve, silly :) I love you so much! !! I can't wait!!! Less than 48 hours, we will be in each other's arms! !! I can't believe I waited this long before I could see you!!!" And this sort of excitability was not limited to one or two students; it was clear that for writers in their age group, e-mail commonly and communally calls for frequent exclamations and shows of animation.

But in addition to recreating, or reinventing, the tone of Evelina's letters, the students often showed real flair for creating epistolary tension. Below is a truncated exchange from a very Richardsonian story of a female student seduced by her substitute Biology instructor. Among other things, note the way in which the subject-heading lines add a kind of schematic outline of the unfolding narrative:

```
Date: Tues 10 Sept 1996 1646 (EST)
From: Andrea@pop.uvm.edu
To: Mari@pop.uvm.edu
Subject: Wait to hear this~

Mari — two days ago I went to meet with my professor
for my biology class. Turns out the real professor had
a baby and we have this young guy standing in for her.
He is so hot! Well last night I was out and I saw him
downtown. I just went over to talk to him for a minute
and I ended up spending the entire time hanging out
with him. . . . Jeff has hardly called me at all lately
so I am just going to go out and have a good time with-
out him. It's my senior year!!! Gotta run — Andrea


Date: Tues 10 Sept 1996 22:25 (EST)
From: Mari@pop.uvm.edu
To: Andrea@pop.uvm.edu
Subject: You better be careful!!!!

Andrea — Do not be stupid!!!!! You and Jeff were
great together! Don't throw it away. Anyway, write to
me tomorrow when you get this message. Good night.
```

```
Date: Wed 11 Sept 1996 09:41 (EST)
From: Andrea@pop.uvm.edu
To: Mari@pop.uvm.edu
Subject: What a night!!!

Mari! I had such a great time last night. John is my
new professor's name and he is so cool! He bought me
drinks all night. . . . I left with John. You are prob-
ably going to lecture me about it — but we had a great
time. He walked me home and we stayed up until 4 am
talking! He kissed me good night but that was it . . .
```

This student does a good job here of quickly creating a clear if simple dramatic irony—in fact, as the chronologies tell us, this part of the exchange occurred within a twenty-four hour period. Like Pamela, whose "young master" begins to be overfond of her following the death of his mother, the biology professor here is clearly registered as a potential villain. He buys "Andrea" drinks "all night," and yet the young woman herself (like Pamela or Evelina) is unable to see the developing catastrophe. And this author has chosen a confidante, "Mari," whose moral sense is sharper and whose warnings speak to the reader's anxieties.

This anxiety grows as "John," the substitute for the "real professor," begins to act in even more questionable ways: "Anyway, John is great. It is a bit weird to be in his class though. I swear that he sometimes looks at me and winks. But that also might be my imagination." Finally, at the catastrophe, the student author moves closer to what Richardson called "instantaneous descriptions," or more dramatic scene-making:

```
Mari — I should have listened to you. I hate JOHN! !!
Today we are sitting in class and in walks this preg-
nant woman! John introduces her to us as his wife,
Heather. I sat there in utter shock. John never even
looked over at me. I am going to kill him. I wanted
to stand up and yell at him right in front of the en-
tire class. Apparently she has been away on vacation
for a while and she got back a bit early so she
thought that it would be nice to come and surprise
him. . . . What should I do, Mari?
```

In good epistolary form, this narrative closes with some final moralizing from Mari, who instructs Andrea that she should "please, just walk away from the situation. . . . My advice would be to tell him never to contact you again." On the whole, this narrative—while somewhat hackneyed in academic subject matter—shows clearly the ways in which students were able to translate the range of epistolary devices into their own conception of electronic mail. They were able to design and produce chronologically condensed and emotionally charged short stories told in letters.

I'll close with one instance in which a student took the epistolary form in an intriguing new direction. In the following exchange, "Amy" is communicating her anguish at the illness of her aunt to her confidante, "Laurie."

```
From: Amy@pop.uvm.edu
To: Lauri@pop.uvm.edu
Subject: It's been an eye opener

I went home yesterday and saw my Aunt Mary for the
first time in a year or so. You remember her right? She
is a happy, energetic elementary school teacher who
refused to retire until they practically kicked her
out. I know that I told you before that cancer had
invaded her liver, but it has now spread. Seeing her
with cancer puts all my petty problems in perspec-
tive. I underestimated the power of cancer and its
rapid growth. I wasn't warned as to what she looked
like now, after months of chemotherapy and sickness.
My eyes filled with tears when I saw her step through
the door with a cane, a little knit hat, and a long
red coat that looked like it was swallowing her.
```

```
From: Laurie@pop.uvm.edu
To: Amy@pop.uvm.edu
Subject: I'm here for you

I am sorry Amy, I didn't realize that your Aunt Mary
was as sick as you now tell me. I know how over-
whelming it can be to see someone you love in pain.
I feel like it is something that we are going to have
to deal with more and more in life and it scares
me . . . I am here for you, I love you kid, and I know
how scary it can be.
```

Apart from the nice writing here, the sober tone and the relatively light hand with such pathos-filled issues, I would point out the way in which the author has set up the progress of the disease itself to structure the plot. And as a counter-balance, we can expect that the relationship between the two young women will strengthen, as the strength of the cancer victim fades. In this way, the exchange dramatizes and foregrounds the essential sense of connectedness that letters foster, the way in which letters bind us to others. But near the end of the narrative, at the crisis, the author takes the exchange in still another new direction:

```
From: Amy@pop.uvm.edu
To: Laurie@pop.uvm.edu
Subject: Forwarded message from alatella@red bu.edu
```

Dear Laurie — This is a forwarded message that I received. I feel that it applies to both of our lives right now. I love you too, Laurie.

Begin Text of Forwarded Message

. . . .

> After a while you learn
> The subtle difference between holding a hand
>   and chaining a soul
> and you learn that love doesn't mean learning
> and company doesn't mean security. . . .
>
> And you learn that you really can endure
> that you really are strong
> and you really do have worth
> and you learn and you learn
> with every goodbye you learn

At the crisis point, the confidante "forwards" to the protagonist an inspirational poem, which has been drifting about the Internet, moving from address to address, killed at some points, but passed on between individual correspondents who find it relevant in some way to their own shared narrative. In this sense, at the story's bleakest moment, the correspondence is opened up to the community as a whole, in much the same way that public funerals help assuage private grief. The heroine's feelings are universalized, and clearly she and her friend draw strength from this diffuse but potent sense of newly-accessible global connectedness.

My acid test for the attractiveness of a given classroom text or assignment is always this: did it produce *more* work from the students than I asked for? The stories of Raymond Carver produce this effect. Assign students five of his short stories, and they will read seven, or ten. Something similar happens when I teach contemporary poetry, and allow them the freedom of free verse. They'll give me two pages of heartfelt verse, and wait impatiently for comments.

But this e-mail approach to the epistolary novel is the only assignment I've ever found that produced more writing on an eighteenth-century topic than was required. A handful of the story sequences I received were 50 percent or 100 percent over the page limit, twenty pages rather than ten. The response was, simply put, unprecedented in my experience, a mark of the fascination students have developed for epistolary forms, ideas, and culture in the wake of electronic mail. To those of us struggling continually to bring to life texts and concepts 250 years old, struggling to hold enrollments in the age of popular culture, it hasn't come a nanosecond too soon.

6

Collective Letters and Classroom Community

Toby Fulwiler

I commonly compose weekly letters to the collective students in my under-graduate writing classes to engage individuals in a dialogue about their writing as well as to promote a strong sense of community within my classroom. Let me describe two variations of this approach in different semesters teaching a senior seminar called "Writing Yourself, Writing the World," a course meant to intro-duce English majors to writing creative nonfiction instead of the interpretative and argumentative papers assigned in most of their undergraduate classes. The first example takes place in a traditional classroom where I wrote in response to student letters to me; the second example takes place in a computer-equipped classroom where I e-mailed collective responses to student paper drafts.

Collective Paper Letters

The major assignment in this section of "Writing Yourself, Writing the World" is the production of a single piece of creative nonfiction—essentially a re-search-based reflective essay of what needs to be, I explain, of publishable quality. Requirements for the students include 1) reading a variety of published essayists from E.B. White to June Jordan, 2) keeping personal journals (which I neither see nor collect), 3) composing weekly essay drafts, 4) publishing their finished essays in an end-of-term class book, and 5) assembling a story portfo-lio—a chronological narrative highlighting excerpts from course papers that tell individual stories of writer growth. In addition, 6) each student writes me a weekly letter.

The letter-writing process is simple: each Tuesday students write and de-liver a letter to me in class (Dear Toby) about issues related to the course read-ing and writing assignments; each Thursday, at the beginning of class, I deliver back a collective letter to the class (Dear Classmates), quoting some of them, answering questions, raising new issues for them to write back to me about (Fulwiler 1997).

In my syllabus I ask that letters address "any issues that arise in class discussion, text readings, or your own writings." Furthermore, I explain that their "class letters are 'public' since I plan to share portions of them with the whole class to stimulate common discussion. If anyone needs to converse with me in private, please see me in person or send an e-mail." The student-paper letters average just under a page a piece; my collective letter back two pages.

The major assignment, to complete one substantial original "publishable" essay over the term, proves to be provocative but more difficult than the students expect, as such pieces are seldom written off the top of the head or solely from memory. Early in the term, I ask students to try out several possible topics before selecting one to revise for the class book. Then, for the rest of the term, I ask each draft to experiment with a new approach: add archival research, interview experts, visit places, write scenes, play with different voices, and so on (Fulwiler 1992).

The resultant multi-voiced, varied-genre essays are interesting, the published class book exciting, and the private journals—so students tell me—useful. But the assignment that makes the greatest difference, that unites the writing, integrates the readings, and creates a sense of community in the classroom, is, without question, the letters—their own to me, my collective letter back. (The following examples include only my collective letters, since these include samples from the student letters.) One of my early letters back to the class began as follows:

```
Dear Classmates,
     Thanks again for writing me thoughtful letters.
I've thoroughly enjoyed — and learned from — our class
meetings so far; your letters let me learn more about
you as individuals — hard to do when all eighteen of
us are together. Let me comment about issues raised
by some of you:

     Peter — The hardest part about the whole process
     is starting.
     Jeremy — Up until now I have been trying differ-
     ent opening paragraphs (by far the most difficult
     part of any paper for me) and seeing how they work.
     Basically, none of them has.
     Dan — I need some advice . . .about tactics or
     techniques for organizing my ideas, for just get-
     ting started.

     You three are not alone; starting is tough — it's
what stops many people from writing at all. The only
secret I know to get over the problem of starting is
to stop worrying about being profound or correct, and
just put some language on paper, and trust that it
```

```
will lead to something good. What I tell my first-year
students is "Plan to throw away the first page" — ad-
vice that takes the pressure off.
```

In all my letters I attempt to set up an empathetic relationship between the students and me as well as the students and each other. Here I've attempted to introduce the whole class to the ongoing conversation among virtually all writers about their struggle to write.

After quoting still other students addressing other composing concerns, this letter concludes by quoting three students who commented on the class itself:

```
Liz — I'm excited to be in a class where I'm encour-
aged to take risks.
Esther — I feel challenged by the group and chal-
lenged to participate and think.
Rachel — I'd like to get to know the people in class
better.

    This seminar is all about risk and experimenta-
tion and taking ourselves (yes, me too) into unfa-
miliar territory and seeing what happens and what
else we can learn. No standing pat until the essays
are published in the class book. So long as we write
and play hard, this class will only get better, more
challenging, more friendly — trust me.
```

The last business I want this letter to accomplish is to increase awareness of ourselves as a community of writers and readers. I also want to acknowledge the unusual nature of the multiple and mandated revisions that make this writing class different from other college classes they've taken before. Whereas most school papers are single-draft, graded-by-the-instructor endeavors, in this class each draft until the final is experimental, and the only grades are those assigned to the mid- and end-term portfolios.

In all my letters I try to keep alive the conversation about our mutual writing processes, to address the difficulties of each experimental draft, and to examine the class atmosphere itself. Here is an excerpt from a letter near the end of the term:

```
Dear Classmates,

    Many of your letters this week forecast the end
of the term and the end of school assignments for a
while. You also acknowledge the hard push yet ahead
of finishing this creative nonfiction essay, publish-
ing it in the class book, and completing your story
portfolio. For instance, Sarah writes: "Are we going
to do another story portfolio? I am trying to figure
```

out my schedule between now and the end of semester —
eleven papers to complete in the next few weeks."

    To which I need repeat, Sarah, yes, the whole idea
of the mid-term story portfolio was to provide practice, a preview, a set of expectations for you to meet
come term's end. So, in reading your final portfolio,
I intend to browse through your drafts, but read your
story portfolio more critically and carefully. Other
concerns:

> Melissa — I'm excited to see how our class book
> comes out . . . really curious about what other
> people have written.
> Joy — I find myself more interested in reading what
> people in our class are writing than in reading the
> established writers.
> Gwen — I am excited. This research is fun.

Throughout the term, students ask me technical questions through the letters—to clarify an assignment that I explained too hastily in class, or to ask advice about completing assignments. When such questions affect the whole
class, I use my return letters to slow me down, to make my expectations understood; in this sense, the classroom letters work as an additional instructional
period, letting me address issues I've forgotten or not covered well in class. In
fact, the planning necessitated in answering each set of letters guarantees a
weekly reconsideration of my class and where it has come so far—the student
letters act, in a loose sense, as a set of weekly course evaluations. In my last letter of the term I decided to ask questions instead of providing answers:

Dear Classmates,
    Thanks for your last letters. Collectively,
you've brought up a number of things that need at-
tending to: How about I ask you some questions back?

> Liz — it's fun to go back and re-read things with
> the insight I've gained in this class. The craft and
> purpose are much clearer now in *everything* I read.
> Jeremey — I have also become a better reader . . .
> reading another student's paper . . . being able to
> come up with concrete suggestions for improving
> it . . . an invaluable addition to the education
> of a college student — even one whose only ambi-
> tion is to visit Graceland!

Hmm. A number of my literature colleagues insist that
the best training to write well is more reading — lots
of reading. Do you think, on the basis of the testi-

mony of Jeremy and Liz, that we can also suggest that
the best training for reading is writing?

   Shana — Is creative nonfiction appropriate for term
   papers?

Good question. Could writing creative nonfiction get
you in a jam in courses that seem to require academic
writing? Does it depend on how you do it? What do you
think professor/readers want, anyway?

   So, those are my questions back, me figuring it's
the time in a course where things pretty much run themselves, where you all have as many (or more) answers
as I have.

I chose to write my last letters as a series of questions, hoping that my
classmates are more confident answerers now than at the beginning of the term.
Still talking about specific assignments, still talking about individual composing processes—but also now addressing questions that affect life beyond this
course: what about finishing? What about using creative techniques to write
more traditional paper assignments? When I delivered this letter at the start of
a Tuesday class, everyone wrote an answer to one or another of my questions,
and we shared those in public for a lively last-class discussion.

   By term's end, everyone in the class agreed that the letter correspondence
back and forth had allowed for a healthy sharing of both ideas and frustration,
had kept everyone apprised of assignment difficulties and expectations, and
had created a trusting community of writers and learners. The added benefit for
me—and by extension my students—is that I became a better teacher. But like
my students, I didn't want to stand pat with this self-assignment, so the next
several semesters I experimented with collective letters electronically, with
mixed though interesting results.

Collective E-mail Letters

The advent of free e-mail accounts for college students makes it possible for
asynchronous (out-of-real time) communication between instructors and students outside of conventional class and office hours. It also makes, I imagined,
hand-delivered paper letters obsolete. Like many college instructors, I embraced
e-mail as the ultimate solution to creating student-student and student-teacher
dialogue outside of class about issues important to the class, so I replaced the
paper-letter system with an electronic system that required each student in my
senior seminar to subscribe to the class listserv in order to share ideas about the
class, reading assignments, writing topics, and the like.

   However, the first time I switched to electronically-delivered letters, the new
process produced neither the ready dialogue nor the quick sense of community
of the old-fashioned method. Some students never succeeded in subscribing to

the class listserv despite what I believed to be crystal-clear directions; many did not regularly check their e-mail, despite strong instructor insistence; those who subscribed and checked successfully wrote briefer and more superficial letters than when they printed out letters on paper; and, perhaps most puzzling of all, no one ever responded to questions I raised in my listserv letters back—no one, in other words, had a genuine dialogue with me.

In my first casual experimental go-round with electronic dialogue, I had forgotten that our shared virtual environment was still school, where voluntary dialogues between student and instructor have less urgency than required quizzes, examinations, and term papers. To make the listserv work, I needed to add an equivalent urgency for subscribing, checking, reading, and responding, so next time, that is what I did.

In last semester's senior seminar, "Writing Yourself, Writing the World," I added urgency: I used the listserv exclusively to send my critical responses to each paper draft to all students in the class. If students wanted instructor feedback on their papers, they needed to check and read their e-mail. The process went like this: When I finished reading each paper draft, I wrote a response to each student by name that accomplished three things: 1) it summarized in one sentence the topic of the paper, 2) it raised critical questions about the topic, and 3) it queried each student about the next topic or form the paper might take. Then, I e-mailed my response to each individual paper to the entire class. In other words, everyone was able to read not only my response to his or her paper, but my response to everyone else's paper as well. Bingo, it worked! Everybody read their e-mail.

In trying to solve the problem of students not taking e-mail letters seriously, I inadvertently solved several other problems I had been only dimly aware of: 1) how to get students to more quickly and completely understand an assignment, 2) how to let everyone know the topics and progress everyone else was making, and 3) how to get responses back to people more quickly than the next class meeting. Before I discuss further implications of this assignment, it would help to read through excerpts from the five collective letters I sent to the whole class.

Topic #1

Dear classmates: This is an experiment in responding to individuals, yet sharing these also with the whole class. I'm trying this process for the first time in the belief that reading what I say to others may circle back and help you as well. Please let me know via individual or listserv e-mail if this is, in fact, helpful, or if you feel compromised with my comments being broadcast to all. Six questions I'll be asking everyone, every draft: 1) Can you identify the question in your subject? 2) Can you see yet both an apparent subject and a deeper one? 3) If you labeled its form, what would it be? 4) What are you learning as you're writing? 5) Why do you think we'll want to read it? And 6) can you imagine working on this piece for five more weeks?

Carolyn describes a ride with her drunken room-mate on a fast motorcycle and watches him get busted by cops. She's not entirely sure what she learned from this or where else to take it. Well, Carolyn, I know the feeling of going fast on a motorcycle, and your description captures it accurately. The question: is there a deeper story behind the apparent story? What would you have us learn from your personal experience that you think we don't already know? What more will you learn by writing more about it? Perhaps topic #2 could originate from curiosity instead of memory?

Emily writes of a painful break-up with a boy-friend who treated her badly and seems obviously to be a jerk. As Emily's prefatory note explains, it's a therapy piece of writing, not intended for further revision, unless she decides to pur-sue a small research piece on writing as ther-apy. My question, Emily, is what next? Instead of exploring your personal past, how about tack-ling a less emotional subject — any ideas?

Daniel describes an encounter one night with a blind person who was lost, and how this encounter caused him to think about the importance of be-ing located in space. Dan, I think there is mate-rial here to work with for a deeper topic, since your memory could be aided by geographic re-search. I also sense a genuine interest here about being lost or located, and how that leads us to a sense of identity and rooted-ness. Let me know where else you might take this.

Topic #2

Dear Classmates: I'm really pleased that most of you have gone out and found something outside yourselves to investigate — good start. Two major problems emerge with a number of the pieces: First, when I asked you to "go out to observe something," most of you went someplace close and handy because

time was tight, so it was necessity rather than curiosity that drove the topic. Second, selecting a topic
about a far-away place with no chance for a real local angle doesn't make too much sense either, since
the writer can only know about it from memory or distant research. For topic #3, keep moving out and away
from yourself, but do so with genuine curiosity.

> Emily now summarizes the difficult life histories
> of several teenagers who inhabit a homeless shel-
> ter in downtown Burlington, speculating on the
> differences between her life and theirs. There's
> a lot crammed into this piece, so nothing yet is
> carefully developed or explained — all you need,
> Emily, is focus and time to make this field re-
> search into a more personal essay.

> Liz writes a Suds and Duds Laundromat paper, ob-
> serving what it is that people do while they
> kill time waiting for clothing to be done. She
> becomes aware that this is a safe setting and
> feels at home here. Topic could expand into an
> essay on spare time or washing/drying or end up
> profiling this single laundromat or the Burling-
> ton laundromat scene. Deeper meanings creep in
> here and there among the spin-dry cycles. Writer
> moves in and out of the paper. Is the writer re-
> ally curious about laundromats, or does she have
> dirty clothes?

Topic #3

Dear Classmates: With a few exceptions, this third
set of topics showed little investment in time, energy, or imagination on the part of class authors. On
the whole, I'd say many of you took a few steps back-
ward. Mid-term slump by week four? An early attack of
senioritis? Whatever the reason, let me remind you to
avoid topics you know too much about already as well
as topics that are too safe and comfortable. Be willing to take some risks with subject, form, voice, and
theme. Be willing to explore topics that are of interest but have unknown dimensions. . . . Following
are my observations on the latest round of topics:

> Josh writes (rather desperately, I presume)
> about "procrastination" — a topic his group as-

sures him everyone can relate to, but about which the author states "I don't want to invest any more time in this topic."

Dave describes a bus ride to and from Boston ($72.25 round trip) including brief snatches of conversation with fellow passengers. While professing interest in writing a real travel narrative, Dave says of this paper "it is the most weakly written on so far."

Topic #4

Dear Classmates: I enjoyed reading this set of topics since most of you went farther afield in search of genuinely interesting topics. Plan to give special attention to the next and last topic, especially if you don't much like any of the previous topics. . . . Think about both published essays we've been reading and about the topics of classmates that most appeal to you as a reader — why do they appeal to you? What equivalent can you find in the local environment? Following are my observations on the latest round of topics:

Barry describes the day he spent at the Burlington International Airport, focusing on his time with an airport operations specialist, which included a truck ride to inspect the runways. So far, no clear focus emerges, but it's clear that the more Barry hangs around the airport, the more chances for a story emerge; next draft could easily be another view of the airport, a profile of another airport worker, a survey of customers, or some other dimension of airport life.

Alison writes of gargoyles here, but so far examines no local examples. Were you to pursue gargoyles, the local dimension would be the ticket to a lively and informative paper — the fact (it seems an odd fact) that gargoyles appear on the old train station in this modest-sized American city, a place so far from the origins and purposes of such ornamentation, is worth wondering and speculating about.

Topic #5

Dear Classmates: I see a fair amount of serious work in pursuing this last possible topic, for which I'm grateful. Some of you know where you're headed next, but some of you still don't. That's why I've suggested our conference for Monday. If you know what you intend to develop, I'd like to hear and explore with you your tentative plans; if you don't yet know your topic, I'd like you to use our conference as yet another deadline to find one — so, bring with you a page or so of another (sixth?) possible creative nonfiction topic, and we'll explore it then and there.

> Liz examines the topic of porches, those places people sit to watch the world go by, to store old refrigerators, and take shelter from the rain. Liz, this is a subject full of potential. Your note tells me you already know you need a tighter focus and an answer to the question: "What about porches?" The fact that you've experience with porches yourself, the fact that they're all over Burlington (not to mention the world), and the fact that you could do historical research and place them in various contexts makes this a rich topic for further exploration.

By sharing each response with everyone, students found themselves helping each other and also getting ideas for new topics from what I quoted or suggested. In addition, the fact that everyone heard not only my question to him or her, but witnessed another version of my question to someone else, made it much clearer what I expected from the assignment; several students told me they began to see both the nature and the pattern of the questions I asked.

If I had anything especially critical or negative to say, I had planned to share that only with the writer in question; however since I respond primarily by asking questions—often leading questions to be sure—I never needed to do that. In sum, I was pleased and most of the students were pleased with this new mode of a collective instructor letter.

How did the students perceive the experiment? By mid-term each student had received five collective response letters from me, a response apiece on each of their five topic possibilities. They communicated their reactions to my responses in a variety of ways, including in-class conversations, e-mail, office conferences, and in how they approached their next topics. For example, when I publicly queried Liz about her laundromat paper (Topic #2), she e-mailed me the following:

```
I had a limited amount of time to decide what to do
this week. Tuesday night I was leaving to do my laun-
dry when I realized that a Laundromat would be an in-
teresting place to people watch: How do people kill
time? How do men launder different from women? How
does this laundromat compare to others? What's dif-
ferent at different times of day?
```

Liz's response back confirmed that I was correct in guessing she had chosen something close and handy, but her questions also convinced me that she could make the topic interesting. As you may have noticed, however, she switched to the topic of front porches (topic #5) and wrote her final essay about that.

It seemed clear to me that this mode of collective public response added a substantial amount of contextual information for the students that had usually been missing from my writing classes—very much the opposite from but complementary to another kind of teaching I believe in, one-to-one conferencing about individual papers. Most of the students concurred, never having experienced this mode of response before:

```
Alison — Your responses over listserv were unbeliev-
ably helpful. They not only satisfied my curiosity in
regards to what topics everyone was writing on in a
given week, but it was helpful to see what problems
others were struggling with — were they the same as
mine.

Daniel — I thought your responses to our writing,
posted on the listserv, worked as a good class gauge.
They told us how we were doing relative to the rest
of the class.

Aliza — I sometimes felt my topics were stupid, but
seeing what others were writing helped me see that
my topic was only stupid if I didn't work at it.

Tim — While I was a little nervous about it at first,
I didn't want public disapproval :), I found that
criticism in public rather than in private makes you
try harder so that you may possibly achieve praise
in that same public.

Kate — I enjoyed the deliciously voyeuristic feeling
each week of reading your comments to other people.
The comment directed at me was helpful, but never as
interesting as the one's pertaining to other people's
```

```
essays. . . . The listserv works well that way — it
fosters a sense of community.
```

At the same time, not every student was pleased. Used to getting paper drafts returned with detailed instructor comments on each page, several students found this method not helpful:

```
Amanda: I was not wild about the e-mail responses.
It was helpful to read what you had to say about oth-
er's writings, but at the same time I was always look-
ing for more feedback from you . . . more personal
criticism.
```

As near as I can tell, I had maybe two or three students out of eighteen who wanted more commentary from me than these long collective letters delivered. Though I would always like to please every student, I actually felt those who wanted detailed comments on first drafts really missed the point. Students are used to an entirely different system of response to their college papers from most instructors—this despite several decades emphasizing process writing within English departments and across the curriculum. Typical assignments are still to be completed in one draft; only the instructor reads the paper; the paper is graded; and the comments back are detailed enough to justify the grade.

However, I never give detailed comments on first drafts of multi-draft assignments—a policy this class of students would not be aware of. In truth, these drafts were so general—a condition I've come to expect with first-draft school assignments—that what individuals received in my collective letter was about the same as I would have written on individual papers. I know that by draft three or four, the sentences, the ideas, often the topic will have changed—so detailed individual commentary is not only a waste of my time, it may actually impede the writer from trying further experiments by focusing too much attention on language not yet ready for such attention. Actually, I think I wrote longer and more careful responses in the collective letter, since I was aware of a larger audience. In addition, I'm making these responses to students after they have shared papers in class with small writing groups and already received peer feedback; I would never want to write so detailed a comment as to override the peer feedback they already received.

During the second half of the term, as students honed in on particular topics in more depth, I stopped writing the collective letter responses and gave ever more specific commentary on each individual paper—including margin comments—and so wrote on the papers in a manner to which all were accustomed. One of the other students, Hillary, who had not liked my collective letters, now seemed more pleased:

```
You know that I did not like the e-mail responses from
you. I felt that it was a cheap way out. Reading a
four-line comment about a paper without any direct
```

```
references to it really did not help me make my pa-
pers any better. I need to 'see' what you liked and
did not like — meaning comments on the paper itself.
Generalized comments brought me no farther than the
paper had itself — I like specifics. I liked it much
better at the end of the semester when you made di-
rect comments on our papers.
```

While I disagreed with Hilary that I had taken "a cheap way out," I agreed that during the second half of the term another mode of response was called for, since the topics deepened and the writers became more concerned about an order, evidence, style, and voice. However, the five weeks of collective letters had established a communal tone that carried over into the second half of the term: students knew each other's topics and empathized with each other's struggles in a way that could not have happened without so much public sharing. At semester's end, Dylan put it this way:

```
There was an intimacy in our class that I've never
had in any class prior — we were a group, aiming and
helping each other develop as writers, a strong con-
nection between the students and you because of the
e-mail — we could always see what each other was say-
ing as well as understand what you were trying to
teach us.
```

Coda

When I wrote weekly collective letters on paper about a variety of class issues that I hand delivered in a conventional classroom, I was convinced that was the best way to create classroom community. Then, when I wrote the series of collective response letters and delivered them electronically to students who met regularly in a computer classroom, I was convinced that was the best way to create classroom community. Next term I may invent yet another system of sharing via collective instructor letters; however, I'm convinced that it will include those elements that made these experiments work: that students gained regular and substantial access to their classmates' voices and struggles and to their instructor's intentions and expectations.

Works Cited

Fulwiler, T. 1992. "Provocative Revision." *The Writing Center Journal.* 12.2: 190–204.

———. 1997. "Writing Back and Forth: Class Letters." In *Writing to Learn: Strategies for Assigning and Responding to Writing Across the Disciplines,* eds. Mary Deane Sorcinelli and Peter Elbow, 15–25. San Fransisco: Jossey Bass.

7

Crossing Bridges to the Academy

Letters in the Composition Classroom

Traci Jersen

> It is in the thrill of the pull between someone else's authority and our own, between submission and independence, that we must discover how to define ourselves. In the uncertainty of that struggle, we have a chance of finding the voice of our own authority. Finding it, we can speak convincingly . . . at long last.
>
> —Sondra Perl

It was my very first year of English graduate school when, amidst seminar papers, all-night research sessions, and long hours in the library, I stepped into a refreshing graduate course, "An Introduction to Rhetoric and Composition" (English 340), at the University of Vermont. It was refreshing that in addition to the usual expected academic research and formal papers, we were asked to write weekly letters to our professor to respond to a variety of readings in composition theory. In the syllabus, the professor addressed us in letter form:

```
Each Tuesday, deliver a letter (a page or so, single
spaced) to me about ideas related to our readings,
writings, or discussions (starting with this first
class). Please make each letter honest, lively, and
as personal as you feel comfortable doing, while still
addressing matters of both intellectual and emo-
tional concern about writing and teaching writing.
```

To respond to the student letters, the professor would write a letter back to our class as a whole every week (Dear Classmates)—answering our questions and addressing our concerns. He would leave them outside his office every Thursday afternoon, and one hour later they would be gone.

I'll admit to being a bit startled, at first, being asked to write informal letters to my professor, but soon I became convinced that this assignment served an important purpose. By addressing the professor directly, we were able to enter into a conversation about our concerns about the class, our personal academic struggles, and our analysis of the course material, allowing us to discover our role, place, and importance in this new community of learners. The syllabus further explained that the letters would be expected on a weekly basis but would not be graded. In other words, we were expected to write the letters but not to worry that what they said would affect our course grade, which would be determined by the quality of three more formal assignments. This chapter examines the role letters played in providing a bridge between the personal situation of three master's candidates and the professional world of English Studies they were preparing to enter.[1]

For my own seminar research project, I wanted to understand what these letters meant to my fellow first-year graduate classmates, and how letters helped them understand their role in both this class and the larger field of composition studies. The more I examined my classmates' letters, the more I became convinced that this assignment provided a bridge between the personal language and expectations with which we arrived in the seminar and the academic language and expectations we, as master's candidates, had set out to learn. Our dilemma as first-year graduate students was similar to that faced by first-year students entering the academy for the first time, as one of our seminar readings discussed. In "Inventing the University," David Bartholomae (1996) analyzes the effect that academic language has on student thinking and writing:

> Every time a student sits down to write for us, he has to invent the university for the occasion—invent the university, that is, or a branch of it, like history or anthropology or economics or English. The student has to learn to speak our language, to speak as we do, to try on the peculiar ways of knowing, selecting, evaluating, reporting, concluding, and arguing that define the discourse of our community. (460)

While novices in any field of study cannot be expected to express ideas with the skill and understanding of the experts in that field, many course assignments—especially in graduate schools—actually make such a request. And when students fail, as often they do, to write their assigned papers in fully schooled academic voices, they are often penalized by harsh criticism and low grades. We might ask: do such assignments invite students to, in essence, "fake" understanding for the sake of sounding intelligent and earning high grades? Lad Tobin addresses this issue in *Writing Relationships* (1993), citing the example of Nikki, who was asked to write a paper using "impeccable English prose" for a humanities professor and complained that, "When I try to write 'impeccable English prose', I lose sight of my audience and I disappear as a writer." Tobin goes on to say:

> Her point is not simply that her expression became more awkward in her humanities papers; instead, she is arguing that in the translation from her own form of expression to the academic language required in that course, her actual ideas were lost or distorted. The irony, she concludes, is that although her humanities teacher claims to value creativity and logic, he insists that students write in a form that virtually guarantees detachment and confusion. (23–4)

The 'detachment' and 'confusion' is evident in student papers that are full of the right vocabulary but are void of opinions or ideas. It is important here to stress that although students may see the inherent academic value this language has, it may not mean much to them on a personal level. This creates a gap or barrier between what is considered valuable and what is considered useful. It is necessary, then, for students to acquire the practical meanings of this language and not simply "try-on" the elevated prose of scholarly writing in order for them to move towards a full understanding of their texts and become proficient in the language that their specific field requires. In "Collaborative Learning and the 'Conversation of Mankind,'" Kenneth Bruffee (1996) explains the normal discourse of the academy as follows: "Normal discourse is pointed; it is explanatory and argumentative. Its purpose is to justify belief to the satisfaction of other people within the author's community of knowledgeable peers" (90). So, how does the student—and again, especially the graduate student—acquire the discourse necessary to move from apprentice to colleague?

The answer in our graduate seminar proved to be letters. This "low-stakes"[2] conversation-inviting assignment gives students the opportunity to tie together material from their reading and from their personal experiences in a non-threatening and productive environment without recourse to faking it. Letters demonstrate their involvement with and understanding of the material of the course, becoming a way to bridge the gap and reveal the "know" without receiving the evaluative and critical "no." The letter assignment allowed us to explore and correct misconceptions and mis-readings and gave us a neutral (non-evaluative) space for intellectual growth. In the three examples of graduate-student letters that follow, the language of the letters provides an indicator of the comfort or discomfort of the writer with the language and ideas of the new discipline.

Writer #1

Lisa is a graduate student of English at the University of Vermont. In her undergraduate education she was an anthropology major; thus, she is already in the course as an "outsider." She describes her feelings to the professor in her first letter, dated January 21:

You may not have noticed, since you don't know me, but my writing voice is very self-conscious . . . I chucked the first paragraph of this letter, it was full of my nervous and self-deprecating reminiscences of the first day of school. I was feeling like an outsider in a close-knit group of graduate students.

Lisa does not engage, as assigned, with the readings for that week, but instead talks about her uncomfortable situation in a class full of English master's candidates. She continues, "my entire posture is devoted to a conflict-free day, and my written words reflect this. I do have the fear that someone will dislike my real voice." While Lisa is uncomfortable with what she is writing versus what she thinks she should be writing, her letter allows her to voice her concern and hesitancy in her own words to her professor, allowing him to see into her insecurities in the classroom. After distancing herself from her fellow students, she ends this letter by writing: "Look, I've already switched to a tighter font than usual so I wouldn't look too wordy." Since the instructor responses to concerns such as these were always reassuring, the letter exchanges worked to progressively relax Lisa's tension at being in the class.

In her second letter, dated January 28, Lisa still writes in a voice that reveals her marginal and insecure status. Speaking of the latest class discussion that focused on the assigned readings, she writes, "I think I missed the point, and didn't end up with the plethora of quotes that came from the other participants." Still regarding herself as a less than fully able participant, Lisa is searching for some approval from the professor through expressing her personal "hopes" that she belongs in this class, "I hope I am keeping up enough in my own participation." As if to demonstrate that she is, in fact, well-educated and quite literate, she uses sophisticated words such as "plethora" and "demystify" as she discusses the readings. While she communicates her discomfort with the class, she also reveals her intelligence and willingness to "try-on" the new ideas and language.

Lisa's trepidation is further illuminated in her fifth letter dated February 18, where she begins with a confident judgment: "I was impressed with the [Min-Zhan] Lu essay. I thought she was remarkably insightful about the development of her consciousness." At the same time, she remains a little wary: "but I was afraid I wouldn't be able to express her ideas to anybody [in class]." In addition, Lisa addresses the readings for the week, again evaluating an author's position: "Likewise, I felt his argument [with the WAC workshop approach] was a little too emotional." Although personally criticizing this published author, most of her letter continues to describe her own mental state as afraid, terrified, and nerve-wracking—indicating, I think, her continuing discomfort with the legitimacy of her opinions and ideas.

Lisa's letters are a window into her academic struggles, a way in which she can be honest with the professor, who might otherwise mistake her fear for hostility, aloofness, or boredom.

Lisa's sixth letter begins not only in disagreement with the reading, but with reasons why. Addressing Lad Tobin's *Writing Relationships: What Really Happens in the Classroom* (1993), where the author expresses and explains his anxieties as a teacher, she writes: "Tobin's book was interesting . . . but I wondered if it would ever mollify this reader . . . it would have helped dampen the embarrassment and criticism I now have for his teaching." There seems to be an advance here over Lisa's stance in the previous letters, as she expresses her own intellectual, I'm-a-part-of-this-discourse-community opinion, reacting against an established, well-respected figure in language close to "normal discourse," apparently comfortable about asserting her opinion against his: "Tobin's self-reflective, hand-writing analysis went round and round in an ineffective fretting that never resulted in solutions or success." In her previous letters, Lisa has usually agreed "wholeheartedly," as she writes in one letter, with the readings, yet her criticism of Tobin's teaching styles suggests a new courage to enter more within a "community of knowledgeable peers." However, by the end of the sixth letter, she has again backed away and returned to her marginalized status: "And I fear that I am going to be the only class member relating this way to the book, and that I am, somehow, because of that reaction, in the wrong. That I will be isolated. Show myself as an outsider." She ends her letter with: "Please don't take offense to my reactions to last week's class and the criticism I have for this Tobin book." Lisa can grapple with the writer in her letter, but is still unable to voice her true opinion in class with confidence and authority. Lisa, afraid to further alienate herself from her classmates, weakens her position as a writer and critic: "I am obviously uncomfortable with this letter." Her disclaimer reveals her inability to tackle the text with any authority. She approaches but cannot cross the bridge from apprentice to what Bruffee considers a colleague, alienated not only from her classmates but from the material she is studying.

In her last letter, dated March 11, Lisa explains most clearly her continued alienation from the rhetoric of the composition discourse community, which has included readings from not only the composition theorists already mentioned, but also from Janet Emig, James Britton, Sondra Perl, Nancy Sommers, James Berlin, Elizabeth Flynn, Patricia Bizzel James Reither, and John Trimbur:

```
This weekly writing allows me the freedom to examine
my reactions to the readings and formulate my thoughts
on current projects without the danger of speaking
out loud for too long . . . but I doubt if I could
voice the ideals above . . . what is up with these
readings? Are you just trying to stir up dissent or
is it only me? They are so frustrating to me. I feel
like I'm not learning anything. . . . I'm probably not
a standard measure of the rhetorician's effective-
ness, but I am often alienated and find myself hyper-
```

```
critical while reading these essays. Why does rheto-
ric have to be so absurd, why can't they put it in
simple, straightforward words?
```

Even though, as Elbow (1997) states, "learning a discipline also means learning not to use that discourse," which Lisa does here, it is also important that "students don't know a field until they can write and talk about what is in the textbook and in the lectures in their *own* lingo, in their informal *home* or *personal* language—language that is . . . saturated with sense or experience"(7). The letters are the place for this informal language, yet Lisa is unable to do this. She cannot address most of the "absurd" discourse that is taking place in the texts with proof that she is somehow involved with the material on a personal level —she simply rejects it. She is frustrated with what she cannot understand and believes she really isn't learning anything. The value of these letters is two-fold. Lisa was so distanced from what she was supposed to be learning that she could not express her ideas or opinions in class—but she could voice her concerns in her letter. And a seminar paper may have been a good way for Lisa to disguise her failure, but by troubleshooting her fears and distrust in the letters, her professor was able to guide her toward completing a successful seminar paper that avoided the lingo with which she was so upset.

Writer #2

Whereas Lisa had trouble developing her voice and comfort level within the composition discipline, Dave, a first-year English graduate student, enters the composition discourse community quickly and with apparent confidence, as evidenced by his first letter dated January 20: "As far as this week's readings go, I found everything written to be relevant and interesting, perhaps even helpful, but I did take issue with a few general things." Dave immediately asserts his opinion on the writers he read that week: "Murray and Bissex's voices read problematically in the area of credibility . . . on the other hand, I really enjoyed Elbow's essay on "real voice" and power. This guy seemed more like a writer . . ." Here, David Bartholomae's analysis of "advanced writers" is helpful, as he suggests they "place themselves both within and against a discourse . . . working self-consciously to claim an interpretive project of their own, one that grants them the privilege to speak" (1996, 475). His letter discourse is a mixture of formal discourse jargon (problematically) and informal talk (this guy). In contrast, Lisa, as we have seen, was unable to adopt such an assertive stance. That is, Dave agrees and disagrees with what he has read, and his letter language suggests a comfort level in so doing. As Dave states in his first letter, after giving his opinions of Murray and Bissex: "I don't know, maybe I require some incomprehensible lingo in order to be suitably impressed as to the voice of authority in an essay." The notion of English academic discourse, or "incomprehensible lingo," is an issue that concerns Dave on a weekly basis. He mocks the idea of fancy rhetoric as a requirement for authority—even as he participates in using some of it himself. Asserting his own critical opinion, Dave states, "this doesn't seem healthy, educating, or self-expressive—what can we do? Let's change it. Instead of rewording vocabulary, strive deeper to the roots of your argument to what you wish your reader to understand, to be convinced of . . . try to say something unique to you, composed your way, not their way." While Dave shows discomfort with the ideas in the essay, he shows little discomfort in positioning himself as a critic of composition studies. Dave shows impatience—even anger—with the lingo of composition studies in his next letter, yet he reflects on what each writer is trying to say and interprets their discussion into his own words:

> James Reither is no Peter Elbow (write like a writer goddam it! Write like you mean it!) But I can see his logic. It extends to all areas of the composition studies discipline. Writing is gradually entering into a space large enough not to be encapsulated in linear thought, so much the way we were "taught" to write.

Dave extends his analysis by offering his own view of the structure of composition studies as a whole. He becomes a critic not only of the language, but of the ideas behind that language, by relating the text to his own experience and investigating deeper into Reither's argument. At the same time that Dave comfortably rails against "these damn critic, educator, theorist, philosopher, intellectual writers?!" he attempts to maintain a valid interpretive perspective. While Dave might be cautioned to give the authors in the new field some benefit of doubt, the letters allow him a venue for what might be called overly-confident assertions just as they allow one for Lisa's more hesitant ones.

Dave's letters also reveal his rebellious academic personality, "I'm not a teacher, I'm a punk-mouthed donkey who's into creative, or completely plagiarized, soundings-off. I'm not very good at being academic, or an intellectual for that matter." Were he to write a seminar paper, it is unlikely we would see this punk side of Dave's voice, but it comes through loud and clear in his weekly letters. At the same time, we witness the effects of his critical reading in his letters—he works against the rhetoric in the essays, while challenging and transforming ideas and language into his own words and methods for writing—which are not always so irreverent as the previous examples suggest. The following passage reveals his own larger and more serious perspective:

> Most of the essays tended to pull away from technical commentaries . . . on everything from voice, to revision tactics, to drafting procedures, and at least attempted to deal with some questions relating to the infamous 'bigger picture' (of writing in gen-

```
eral, and in some cases, the discipline under delib-
eration: composition studies).
```

Dave does not use the "incomprehensible lingo" of English academic study, but he often stabs at the heart of the essays he reads with his own rhetorical flourish. He interacts with the readings and shares that interaction with his professor. For someone who claims not to be "very good at being an academic," his continuous banter with established professionals in his field, his faith in himself as a writer, and his creative flair for profanity and cynicism suggest he's well on his way toward Bruffee's "colleague" status. As Dave puts it, "In order to begin to read, understand, write . . . you must learn a new language to be accepted."

Dave's letters reveal a graduate student's attempt to connect personally to each of the assigned academic readings, allowing him to locate his own niche in the intellectual world he is about to enter. The letters suggest that, unlike Lisa, Dave is able to find practical applications for some of the new knowledge, even as he dismisses the language in which much of it is couched. The letters provide a vehicle for working through his immediate visceral reactions to the readings; he neither accepts the jargon of the new discipline nor fakes writing in it himself. As a mastery of the discourse is required to be fully part of an intellectual community (Bruffee 1996, 90), the letter assignment allowed Dave to create a bridge between his past experience as a writer and theoretical discussion of writing he found in the course readings. Thus, by moving comfortably within and against the discourse, a student emerges as a "colleague."

Writer #3

Aaron, a first-year English graduate student who is also a teaching assistant with a semester of first-year composition already under his belt, already sees himself as a participant within the composition discourse community. At the same time, he struggles with the theoretical nature of the readings within the discipline. In his first letter, dated January 20, Aaron identifies with writers like Glenda Bissex as a teacher: "Bissex argues exactly what I urge: show your writing . . . I try to emphasize to my class the 'social nature of writing.'" In addition, Aaron initially reveals a competence that eludes Lisa and Dave: "I've read Faigley's article before, and I frankly still don't understand what his synthesis entails. He calls it historical awareness, but he really doesn't provide examples that would clarify. . . . it seems so broad and tedious." He also tests what he reads against his own classroom experience and finds discrepancies: "Reither encourages his students to write with an awareness of how others in the field write . . . but many of them are just freshmen, and thus not ready to join such a level of discourse that Reither favors." Aaron's struggle seems to arise from the overly theoretical nature of readings such as Reither's that do not give him a tangible, useful means of implementing strategies in his own classroom. Aaron

uses the letters to arrive at some sort of understanding that will eventually allow him to fully equate himself with the advanced rhetoricians he is studying.

In order to get to this point, Aaron must be able to grapple with ideas on a
personal level and eventually assimilate this knowledge into his newly adopted
academic life. He begins to do this in his next letter: "I think that each author's
rejection of jargon and such really appeals to me." Aaron is aware that the elevated language of a text potentially shuts him out of a full understanding and
thus a thoughtful analysis of the material. Like Dave, he attempts to get there
by varying degrees, but looks to texts written in his own familiar language to
guide him: "This essay also made me even more convinced that conferences are
great. . . . Annie Dillard's piece portrays writing as a kind of freedom and learning experience, which is really inspiring to me." He still questions what he cannot understand: "But as with the 'jargony' theories of Faigley and Reither, how
does one impress these ideas on students who take the class because it is a requirement?" Aaron, like Dave and Lisa—and virtually all of us in the seminar—rejects their jargon and attempts to find which writers and ideas he wants
to aspire to and identify with, in addition to trying to find a practical means of
applying abstract theories. He openly works through his ideas in his letters and
states, "I am the one who is struggling now, but that is good."

In addition to incorporating ideas from the readings, Aaron finds the professor's advice practical: "I share many of your feelings about collaborative
learning. Obviously as an English 001 instructor who encourages writing in a
classroom community with weekly workshops, I have some vested interest in
these matters." Like Dave, Aaron here looks for a connection between what he
learns and his life—in this case his own composition classroom. He says of his
students:

```
They are most certainly a part of a discourse commu-
nity of writers. But are they really becoming a part
of the academic discourse? I wonder . . . shouldn't
I address the 'gap' between the discourse they learn
in my class and that of the larger institution? I am
not at all interested in placing academic discourse
above what I am teaching. In fact, I don't know that
this 'gap' is as great as I am making it out to be.
```

Here, Aaron seems to be personally maintaining his distance between that "discourse" and what is real. He adds, "this book renews my interest in this field,
an interest that is not really excited by jargon like that of Bruffee . . . but Tobin
tackles a lot of issues very intelligently without the jargon . . . HE'S SPEAK-
ING ABOUT PRACTICAL MATTERS!!"

Aaron's subsequent rejection of "advanced jargon" says a lot about his
place in the realm of English studies. He engages in an intelligent dialogue
through his letters with authors such as Don Murray and Lad Tobin, and is able
to apply practically what he has learned. Through the letters, Aaron voices his

opinions about the highly theoretical writing and is able to come to terms with the issues he struggles with without having to impress the professor with unnecessary "jargon." He is able to apply his readings to a classroom situation and in this way fully make use of his knowledge: "My immediate reaction to the book is of increased awareness in my own personal life. . . . I feel very strongly now about the importance of making those personal connections relate to writing and teaching." Aaron has made the important connection between the personal and academic through these letters, and has taken it one step further—incorporating the material he learns into his own teaching, which he reveals in his last letter:

> I mentioned earlier that I thought these letters were an excellent way to blur the line of academic and personal writing. Bartholomae and Elbow try so hard to reason why the distinctions are there. I am much more interested in seeing how the best of both worlds could happen, how the distinctions could be complicated. The letters in the class really seem to accomplish this. Might not these letters be used to an end that was somewhat academic? This is what I think your use of letter writing does . . . to use the personal and to demonstrate academic discourse as well.

Here, Aaron reveals what the letter assignment actually did for him as well as the rest of us in this graduate seminar: it gave us a friendly venue in which to explore the scholarly frames of mind and habit needed to continue with advanced study. It also gave our professor a way to gauge what we were actually learning inside his classroom. The letters—the fact that we had to articulate our concerns, questions, and insights in written language each week—made a real difference. According to Mike Rose, the act of writing

> assumes a richer epistemology and demands fuller participation. It requires a complete, active, struggling engagement with the facts and principles of a discipline, an encounter with the discipline's texts and the incorporation of them into one's own work, the framing of one's knowledge within the myriad conventions that help define a discipline, the persuading of other investigators that one's knowledge is legitimate. (1996, 457)

Although each student will benefit differently and to varying degrees from letter writing, its significance lies in that this informal, somewhat comfortable writing is a beneficial pedagogical tool for assessing involvement within a discipline. In looking at the three students studied here, it is apparent that the letters served the purpose of allowing students to express insecurities, ideas, and connections. Whereas Lisa may have been uncomfortable stating her opinions in class, she was able, through her letters, to reveal the difficulties she was having with the readings and the class. Without the letters, a professor may have marked her as an ambivalent student. With low-stakes writing, the student can reveal the true learning process without the risk of a bad grade. Because of this, the student is more open to learning and exploring and will be more likely to make a connection in the future by working out ideas and not simply restating them.

Aaron and Dave are good examples of students for whom the bridge function of the letters worked. They used these letters to create a comfortable space for working through personal and academic concerns. Each demonstrated substantial learning along with real questions about that learning. When students can do this successfully, they have become what Bruffee considers a "colleague."

By studying these letters analytically—which I was not able to do while a participant in this class—I was able to discern more clearly both how the letters functioned for the students in class and what the professor was attempting by making the letter assignment. I learned that for most students, these letters were not only valuable, but an assignment they looked forward to every week. From the professor's point of view, the letters allowed a "reading" of the students in a way that neither more formal assignments or classroom discussion ever could. In my last letter to the professor, I wrote the following:

> As a member of this class, I was skeptical of the letter-writing assignment. I kept wondering, where are these letters going to take me? What does the professor want to know about me? In retrospect, though, I realize the value of these letters and the reason why I will use this format with my own students — it is all about *me*, the student. These letters have provided the space for the articulation of the development from a borrowed voice to a reaffirmation that my own voice can exist in academic circles, and I am finally able to claim myself as a writer, a scholar, and finally a teacher. In struggling to find my own voice and not using the voice of "the academy" I have found a place to strengthen my ideas, strengthen my writing, and my critical thinking.

Not only did these letters prove valuable to me as a graduate student, but they proved to be a remarkable tool when I began teaching composition myself, the next year. I adapted the idea myself for my first-year composition students and found the idea worked equally well in bridging the gap between the language of the students' previous lives and the language they were now expected to learn and use as college undergraduates. My students were able to communicate their ideas and concerns to me, and I was also able to assess my own strengths and weaknesses as a teacher and was constantly changing my methods and syllabus to reflect the needs of my students. In short, I've learned to appreciate the power of informal letters to contribute to learning from the perspective of both student and teacher.

Notes

1. I am indebted to Kim Caterino and Kate Rainey for their insightful contributions to this essay.

2. I draw on Peter Elbow's (1997) definition of "low-stakes writing" here: "frequent, informal assignments that make students spend time regularly reflecting in written language on what they are learning from discussions, readings, lectures, and their own thinking" (7).

Works Cited

Bartholomae, D. 1996. "Inventing the University." In *Composition in Four Keys: Inquiring into the Field,* eds. M. Wiley, B. Gleason and L. Wetherbee Phelps, 460–79. Mountain View, CA: Mayfield.

Bissex, G. 1996. "Growing Writers in Classrooms." In *Composition in Four Keys: Inquiring into the Field,* eds. M. Wiley, B. Gleason and L. Wetherbee Phelps, 34–9. Mountain View, CA: Mayfield.

Bruffee, K. 1996. "Collaborative Learning and the 'Conversation of Mankind.'" In *Composition in Four Keys: Inquiring into the Field,* eds. M. Wiley, B. Gleason and L. Wetherbee Phelps, 84–97. Mountain View, CA: Mayfield.

Elbow, P. 1996. "How to Get Power Through Voice." In *Composition in Four Keys: Inquiring into the Field,* eds. M. Wiley, B. Gleason and L. Wetherbee Phelps, 62–7. Mountain View, CA: Mayfield.Wiley.

———. 1997. "High Stakes and Low Stakes in Assigning and Responding to Writing." In *Writing To Learn: Strategies For Assigning and Responding to Writing Across the Disciplines,* eds. P. Elbow and M. Sorcinelli. San Francisco: Jossey-Bass.

Faigley, L. 1994. "Competing Theories of Process: A Critique and a Proposal." In *Landmark Essays on Writing Process,* ed. S. Perl, 149–64. Davis, CA: Hermagoras.

Fulwiler, T. 1997. "Writing Back and Forth: Class Letters." In *Writing To Learn: Strategies For Assigning and Responding to Writing Across the Disciplines,* eds. P. Elbow and M. Sorcinelli. 15–25. San Francisco: Jossey-Bass.

Lu, M-Z. 1994. "From Silence to Words: Writing as Struggle." In *Landmark Essays on Writing Process,* ed. S. Perl, 165–77. Davis, CA: Hermagoras.

Murray, D. 1996. "Teaching the Other Self: The Writer's First Reader." In *Composition in Four Keys: Inquiring into the Field,* eds. M. Wiley, B. Gleason and L. Wetherbee Phelps, 50–55. Mountain View, CA: Mayfield.Wiley.

Perl, S. 1994. "Understanding Composing." In *Landmark Essays on Writing Process,* ed. S. Perl, 99–107. Davis, CA: Hermagoras.

Rose, M. 1996. "The Language of Exclusion: Writing Instruction at the University." In *Composition in Four Keys: Inquiring into the Field,* eds. M. Wiley, B. Gleason and L. Wetherbee Phelps, 445–59. Mountain View, CA: Mayfield.

Reither, J. A. 1994."Writing and Knowing: Toward Redefining the Writing Process." In *Landmark Essays on Writing Process,* ed. S. Perl, 141–8. Davis, CA: Hermagoras.

Tobin, L. 1993. *Writing Relationships: What Really Happens in The Composition Classroom.* Portsmouth, NH: Boynton/Cook.

8

Rehearsal Space

*Working with Correspondence Pairs
in the Graduate Classroom*

Lisa Schnell

Letter-writing involves a complicated acknowledgement of "old"
ideas and new information. It's kind of like ballroom dancing on
paper—a respect for a partner's movement, the belief in one's feet,
and the love of the dance itself.

Megan, student in English 360

Remembered Conversations

In the nine years I've been a college professor I've read countless papers on undergraduate pedagogy; I've even written a couple myself. This makes sense:
when we think of ourselves as classroom teachers, most of us think of the undergraduate classroom and its challenges. To a large extent, this is as it should
be—the undergraduates are, by far, our largest constituency and they represent
some of our most intractable (and tractable) pedagogical subjects (something
that most of the essays in this book will testify to). But for those of us teaching
at colleges that have a graduate program, the undergraduate bias in pedagogical studies can tacitly lead some of us to a kind of complacency with our graduate-student pedagogy that is borne out of a set of unexamined assumptions
about our students. It is so easy, when we encounter what for me is the deeply-
felt *relief* of teaching a roomful of very motivated students, to relax our pedagogical muscles and simply let the students' own interests carry the day.

But graduate students, as most of us remember only too well from our own
graduate-school experiences, have whole closets full of anxieties about their
status in the classroom. And while it is not our role to be therapists to our stu-

dents, we do nonetheless need both to acknowledge and then productively to accommodate some of those anxieties in our graduate pedagogies. It was a truly disappointing experience with a graduate seminar a few years ago that led me, in the weeks preceding the spring semester of 1998, to try to name the anxieties that had frayed my previous experience with graduate teaching. As I reflected back on my own graduate-seminar experiences, I remembered with some discomfort the agony of professional impersonation. Without exception, the assignments in every graduate seminar I took consisted of an oral presentation and a big term paper. There's a good reason why this was, and for the most part still is, so: as professional academics our scholarly lives are measured in oral presentations and big papers; we were apprentices. But most of us were not, nor did we want to be, disciples. So the anxiety involved mastering, for ourselves, a professional discourse, *becoming* an academic. Some few bold souls rehearsed those languages with their professors in intense one-on-one sessions during office hours; most of us rehearsed with each other.

In the Spring of 1998 I was scheduled to teach a graduate seminar called "The King James Bible and Literary Study." I approached the course with not a little trepidation, knowing that not only was I going to encounter professional anxiety in this course, but that I was also going to be dealing with a whole lot of *personal* anxiety: it's an intimidating book to which almost everyone brings a great deal of personal baggage. I knew it could quite easily be a recipe for disaster. My goal was thus, without discarding the oral presentation and the final paper, to devise some sort of *other* writing assignment, an ongoing activity that would, ideally, become a kind of "rehearsal space." And though I wanted to be able to sit in on the rehearsals, I didn't want to direct them. Taking as my inspiration, then, the enormously productive and on-going conversations I had with my own graduate-school peers, I came up with an assignment that I introduced to my students as follows:

> Friends of mine own a beautiful old Tudor home in a suburb of Boston. One of the distinguishing features of their home is the way it seems to be about three or four houses that have been sort of glued together. In fact, it started as a small Tudor-style home in the 1890s, and as the family grew, they added addition after addition until it had become what it was when my friends bought it — an eccentric single building with various wings, up and down. But as odd as it is, it works. It is truly a wonderful home — big and comfortable, full of beautiful details (which bear the varied signatures of the various generations that built each subsequent addition) and architectural insights, eccentric but coherent.

```
     It will help to think of this assignment as a
little like that fabulous house. You will be divided
into letter-writing pairs and will write back and
forth throughout the semester about the reading for
the week ahead and any extra (reserve) reading you
have done. Always bring two copies of your letters
with you to class — one for your partner, one for me
(the silent partner).
     Perhaps the most important thing to remember is
that these are letters (not formal papers, but not
e-mail either). And like any good letter, each one
should be well-written, but full of ideas: some of
those ideas you will want to spin out at some length;
some may just be flashes that you need more time to
think about. The letters should be interesting, en-
gaging, experimental (risky even) — give your part-
ner something to respond to. But make sure you don't
think of each letter as a separate piece of writing
unto itself. At the end of the semester, the two of
you should have a collection of letters that, like
my friends' eccentric house, has an odd but unmis-
takable kind of architectural integrity. And that
doesn't mean that it's "done" — even my friends think
of adding on yet again.
```

In order to stay true to my experiment, I needed to insist on a position that initially, and a little ironically, caused a great deal of anxiety in my students: I would remain silent, an eavesdropper, reserving my comments on their correspondence for the end of the course, when I would evaluate the correspondence as a whole.[1] To be sure, part of the impulse for that had also to do with the subject matter of the seminar and my own place in that room: they would see me as an authority, certainly, but with the Bible I realized that if I didn't disrupt that idea a little bit, I would end up doing far too much talking. I was also curious about the different ways the correspondences would go if there were no "normative" voice interfering with comments and, especially, grades.

In the interests of academic honesty, I should say that anything that looks like genuine foreknowledge of the real possibilities of this assignment is only a kind of optical illusion, the effect of looking back over a memorable graduate seminar and reflecting on what it was that made it so successful. For while it is true that I was consciously revisiting my own graduate experience in constructing the letter-writing assignment for this course, I was mainly oblivious to the enormous possibilities of the assignment. It was only five or six letters into the assignment that I began to be aware of how, in allowing a forum—within an actual graduate course—for the expression of some of the "vocational anxiety" that I recognised from my own graduate-school experience, I had also quite inadvertently stumbled onto an assignment that could accommodate many different learning styles without inducing a kind of schizophrenia into the seminar room.

But before I explain how my expectations were met and, more importantly, *exceeded* over the course of the correspondences I read, I need to touch on what is probably the most daunting, and potentially messy, part of this assignment, and that is the establishment of the correspondence pairs. Before any of the letters were exchanged (but particularly now that I've seen the assignment in action), it was clear that the success of such an exercise depended on there being a certain "chemistry" between the partners. In other words, I knew I could not assign partners alphabetically and achieve the results I was imagining. I used three resources to find that chemistry. The first was my own intuition: I didn't assign pairs until after the second three-hour session. That gave me six hours to collect first impressions (I had taught only one of these students before). Secondly, I asked them to submit to me a totally confidential list of three people they thought they could work with and a list of any of the people they thought they absolutely could not work with. I promised to shred their lists once I'd read them. The lists were enormously helpful (and I did shred them). Thirdly, once I'd drawn up a tentative list of pairs, I took it to a colleague who had taught almost all of these students the previous semester. I asked her not to comment in any substantive way but only to tell me if there was any pairing on the list that she thought would not work. It was a good system and although some of the pairs were inevitably more productive than others, none failed.[2]

Academic Reconnaissance

Steve and Jason formed the most rigorously, even stubbornly, "intellectual" correspondence pair in the class. Both of them were fresh from a critical theory seminar the semester previous and were anxious to try out the radical forms of scepticism they had encountered in that class. In fact, my knowledge of their mutual interest in literary theory led to the pairing; quite frankly, I was worried that either one of them—despite their obvious good natures—might intimidate a partner less committed to the languages of theoretical discourse or, perhaps even worse, that with other partners the two of them would have to compromise their interests entirely in the interests of a mutual exchange. But the success of this pairing has more to it than a basic compatibility of interests. Indeed, perhaps the primary reason this correspondence worked so well has to do with the fact that, as intellectual (and occasionally jargony) as the converse was, both Jason and Steve fully embraced the correspondence as a place to try out ideas. Witness Steve, in what is a fairly typical passage:

```
As far as "correct" readings are concerned, on a ba-
sic level I am of the inclination that this is partly
```

a non-issue since we are always trapped within ideological constructions in the way we understand anything and the very fact that we can make sense at all
out of a text like the K[ing] J[ames] B[ible] indi-
cates that we operate from a set of ideological assumptions whether we are willing to call them such
or not.

   *I don't entirely agree with what I have just writ-
ten,* but I do think it is important to not have any
illusions about the fact that we are reading a 17th-
century text.

   OK so that is enough for me on correct interpretation — it is all just interpretive ideology and context — *always has been and always will be independent
of what the text is.* (my emphasis)

A little like John's Pilate, who refuses to revise the inscription over Jesus's head, saying "what I have written I have written" (John 19:22), Steve's brusque certainty, and his unwillingness to rewrite his dogmatic view about literature and ideology, is nonetheless visited by a wonderful moment of possibility—"I don't entirely agree with what I have just written." I tell my students that, as well-crafted as I expect the letters to be, I don't expect them to do any substantive revising—the letters should be a place where they watch their ideas take shape, where they become aware—as Steve clearly has here—of the effect of *writing something down.* Critical dogmatism, as you've no doubt already guessed, is precisely Steve's problem. While he is not exactly uncomfortable in the role of ideologue, he is well-aware that the exaggerated position he takes on certain issues is getting in the way of his learning. I loved that in this very early letter he puts that self-awareness on display in the form of both an admission and a challenge: he is inviting Jason to engage him on this issue. And where a less confident student might shrink away from Steve's challenge, Jason takes him up on it.

   In his response to this letter of Steve's, Jason's first order of business is to engage Steve on the interpretation issue:

I want to avoid the tendency to argue for one defini-
tive meaning for any text, especially the KJB. As a
result, in order to have a correct reading, we must
have an "intellectually honest" reading. One must
learn to identify and note the ideological assumptions that form any reading. That is, in your response, I don't think you acknowledge the fact that
history and context are interpretations that are not
liberated from ideological constructions.

A first-year graduate student, Jason is not yet ready to take Steve on with a fully-developed argument of his own. (Steve is a little older and has been in the program a little longer.) Jason's points are well-taken; but while he shows some confidence in his thinking, it's also clear that what he's doing here is trying on the costume of the serious, contentious academic, a role that Steve is already much more practised at, more comfortable in. Jason's tentativeness about assuming the role of the hard-edged intellectual, the contentious academic, comes out remarkably clearly—though I think mainly unconsciously—later in this same letter. Reflecting on the character of the Hebrew Bible's God—Yahweh—Jason ends his letter with the following thought:

> One final note, in Judges God makes pseudo-alliances with enemies of the Hebrews so that they may be "delivered." The alliances in themselves are troubling enough with respect to the jealous nature of Yahweh. However, the metaphor of delivery interests me more. There is this notion that the Israelites will be brought out of travail and they are. Yet, they repeatedly fall back into oppression. What type of deliverance is this? *In terms of pedagogy (because that is what I assume this is), there has got to be a better way for God to teach his people.* Maybe I am too compassionate and sappy. (my emphasis)

It's Jason's move to pedagogy that makes his concluding passage so interesting. He is asking a question about *himself.* It renders transparent what I was starting to notice about all the letters: that they were allowing the letter-writers to voice their own professional concerns, though often in unconscious ways.

As Steve's and Jason's correspondence continued to take shape over the semester, Steve's dogmatic approach to the text starts to soften and Jason's confidence grows exponentially. While undoubtedly this has a lot to do with what is going on *outside* the letters, the letters are providing a space in which to rehearse these new positions. And the response each gets from his partner is clearly also contributing to the transformation. Throughout the correspondence Jason responds generously and often interrogatively to issues that may have been originally staked out rather too unbendingly by Steve. As a result, Steve is able to see the possibilities that are opened up by other approaches to the text. Here's a particularly lucid example of this from a letter Steve wrote about two-thirds of the way through the semester:

> At the risk of great hypocrisy I will say that I was a big fan of Ecclesiastes and not just the bit done by the Weavers and the Byrds. I have a sense that part of the reason that I liked this book is that unlike most people I guess I really don't get off so

```
much on play or narrative so much as I do with say
lyrical poetry. Now, yes I am leaving aside the ide-
ological aesthetic construction argument for a while.
```

He's qualifying this aesthetic evaluation like mad . . . *but he says it.* And given Steve's fully committed Marxist position on the power of language to shape consciousness, even this over-qualified assertion *counts.* Even more than when he's asserting his own positions, though, the increasing flexibility of Steve's response to the text shows up in the enthusiastic way in which he engages with the issues brought up by Jason. In the same letter I have quoted above, Steve says to Jason, "Anyway, you are right that we may be beating the old ideological construction issue to death. *Having said that,* I am sort of glad that I have the opportunity to write about Job, Ecclesiastes and Proverbs" (my emphasis). The passage I quoted above follows. Notably, his "having said that" does not signal a turning back to the ideological issues he has been hammering away at (something we might assume that phrase to mean) but is, instead, an acknowledgement of the ways in which Jason, in the letter that immediately precedes this one, had gently turned the now-tired issue of "correct reading" toward other possibilities and *enabled* Steve to pick up other issues himself, even issues to do with aestheticism. "I'm done with the issue of correct reading," Jason had written, "but I am hip to the idea that we may have to create a new 'interpretive community' to get through this text."

Of course, as well as facilitating his own critical experiments, Steve's generous responses to Jason have a real effect on his partner's own emerging critical self-portrait. Let me turn to a late letter, where I am particularly struck by a passage in which Jason discusses Paul's letters from the New Testament. Like his move to God as pedagogue in the passage I quoted above, the self-reflexivity in this passage—though almost certainly unconscious—is obvious:

```
For one thing, the letter as a genre enables the
writer to express consciousness. In [the Letter to
the] Romans, Paul writes, "For that which I do I al-
low not: for what I would, that do I not: but what I
hate, that do I" (7:15). We haven't seen this before
which attests to the ability of the letter genre to
open up possibilities for the writer to tell their
own story. (my emphasis)
```

It may be impossible to decipher what it is that Paul is saying about "his own story," but it is clear what Jason is saying. Jason's "own story" is the story of his academic coming-of-age. Though a lot of work outside of the letters went into his growing self-confidence, I know that the ways in which Jason told his own story in his exchange with Steve—and indeed, the ways in which Steve allowed and supported that—contributed in significant ways to Jason's noticeable academic growth during the semester.[3]

Out of interest, and at the insightful suggestion of one of my colleagues, I asked both Steve and Jason, a full year after completing the course (and after I'd finished the penultimate draft of this paper) to write me each a letter that revisited their experience of the correspondence assignment: thinking retrospectively, how would they evaluate the effect of that particular assignment on their academic life? Although both of them knew their correspondence was the subject of a paper I was writing about letters in the graduate classroom, neither one of them had any idea what I had actually said about them. Steve's letter to me is a somewhat unfocused collection of reflections on the assignment—because I had been deliberately vague about what I wanted in the letter he rather anxiously tries to cover it all. He does confirm my own sense of what I have been calling his "dogmatism": "I was . . . focused on a closed dialogue . . . that was (possibly) a little histrionic just for the sake of the dialogue." He also talks a little about how he responded to Jason in a way that very much confirms my sense of his intellectual generosity: "Jason had to make those tough decisions about what to focus on and, I think, he always chose aspects of the reading that were not first on my list of priorities so it was good to see where he would choose to take things." Jason, however, is much more direct in his reflections and, interestingly, gives a little extra insight into Steve's retrospective along the way:

> I guess I'll start my response by referring to a conversation between Steve and me the other day. Steve mentioned that the nature of the assignment, specifically the fact that we were being graded on the exchange, *enabled or required a bit of academic posturing*. I'd agree with this assessment. . . . Although, I'm not sure if this posturing was necessarily detrimental. For one thing, the assignment did give me an *opportunity to practice finding and then donning a critical persona*. (my emphasis)

Concluding his letter with a reference back to some of the comments I wrote on their correspondence at the end of the course, Jason says,

> I think you are right to note my working from Steve's shadow and the ways that I struggled to come to my own critical identity over the semester (issues I continue to think about in the present). Yet, I begin to wonder if I would have found these things out on my own over time, Maybe this was one of the real values of the correspondence — *speeding up the discovery of self, forcing me to articulate my position very early in my graduate school career*. (my emphasis)

The Personal Is Intellectual

The correspondence between Steve and Jason is notable partly for the *absence* of explicit personal narrative—they make it a priority to stick to the intellectual issues at hand. But this was not the case in some of the other pairs, where an abundance of personal writing characterised the exchange. In one or two cases, I had to steer students gently away from a *reliance* on personal storytelling. But with at least one pair I was aware that, as personal as the narrative might sometimes have become, it was—a bit like good therapy—freeing up the necessary space for productive intellectual reflection. The students in this particular pair—Erin and Rebecca—were, though no less "smart" than Steve and Jason (all four students did "A" work in the more formal parts of course), less sure of their academic selves. While I don't have the space here to speculate on the important (perhaps even urgent) reasons for that—that would be the topic of an entirely separate paper[4]—I do want to spend a moment or two with Erin's and Rebecca's correspondence as a way of demonstrating that, though overly self-indulgent personal narrative should probably be discouraged at an early stage, the aim for graduate correspondence should not necessarily be letters that are uniformly, single-mindedly "intellectual" in content. This might be particularly true in a program like Vermont's, a terminal M.A., in which only a handful of the students are likely to go on to Ph.D. programs. While both Erin and Rebecca were capable of going on, neither one of them was at all sure that that was what she wanted to do after finishing the M.A. And this anxiety crept into the letters. Both women, good friends before the class even began (something I wasn't entirely aware of when I assigned the pairs), often began their letters to each other by talking about their academic anxieties: What did they really think about spending time learning about literary theory? Were there ways to connect their academic interests to the concerns of their "real lives?" Did they imagine a life for themselves inside the academy? While I like to think that the correspondence may have helped them work through some of these anxieties, what I became most interested in as the correspondence developed was the ways in which the prefatorial discussions in the letters seemed, not really surprisingly, to free them both up to the tough literary work the course required.

In a long letter that is ostensibly about the Book of Job, for instance, Rebecca writes at length in her opening few pages about her own melancholia surrounding a career impasse at which she finds herself: "You see, I had been exploring my career options and felt that what would make me really happy and be really rewarding would not be going on for a Ph.D., but rather being a political activist in California for Latinos. . . ." Yet, she goes on to say, what is the point of that if, even with people like Cesar Chavez, Zapata, and Pancho Villa willing to give their lives to fight oppression, people are still oppressed and oppressing? "Even God plays favorites," she says. For Rebecca, herself a Latina, these are *intensely* personal issues and I begin to feel a little *too* much like an eavesdropper as I read this letter. But then she moves her focus to Job, and some remarkable literary work begins to take shape:

> I think of Abraham and how he seemed so willing to
> sacrifice Jacob. Didn't he ask the questions Job asked?
> I feel that in retrospect, Abraham and other charac-
> ters are presented as two-dimensional because they
> accept everything, while Job is one of the few who
> seems real because he asks "real" questions and chal-
> lenges God in a way that other characters are not
> given agency so to do. WOW. I just had a moment of en-
> lightenment, This book is about the complexities of
> people and not about the complexities of God. . . .
> This week's reading gives us a glimpse of what the
> "thinker/intellectual/scholar-type" worries about
> in life. It's like a novel. Each character has dif-
> ferent and important characteristics or the charac-
> ter personifies something we need to pay attention to.

It's much easier to see the way in which the personal becomes the intellectual here than it was with either Jason or Steve Rebecca's letter allows me a glimpse into the anatomy of that transformation; more than that, the letter gives Rebecca a way into "relevance." She may not be solving her career dilemma, but she is, for the moment, fully invested in the intellectual challenge of the course. Rebecca's "moment of enlightenment," as she calls it here, would gain in coherence as the course went on, finally resulting in an ambitious, theoretically sophisticated term paper about the ways in which Bakhtin's theories of the dialogic imagination suggest the Bible's understanding of wisdom as we encounter it in the Book of Job.

While Erin, too, worries in her letters about what she will do after the M.A., she appears more anxious about the present moment and particularly about her relationship to literary theory. If Jason and Steve are busy trying on all kinds of different theoretical costumes, Erin is deciding whether she wants to put her arm in a sleeve at all. Her letters to Rebecca consistently show her trying on a little theory and then quickly putting it aside; as the semester wears on, she becomes bolder in this theoretical "rehearsal space," lingering a little longer each time. In a letter close to the end of the course, for instance, Erin begins to experiment with some of the post-structuralist possibilities of the preface to the Book of John ("In the beginning was the Word . . ."). She begins by mentioning Jacques Lacan's idea of the "imaginary," a concept I had introduced to her during an office visit. She knows she's on to something, but, as she apologises to Rebecca, she knows "this is confusing." After only about four lines, she abandons her line of thinking. The theory is difficult, to be sure, but she is a very good student—I think it's mainly a matter of her not knowing whether she *wants* to be doing this or not. She spends a few short paragraphs doing the literary equivalent of catching her breath—writing about a few inconsequential things that have gone on in class—and then a page later she steps back in to the discussion she had earlier abandoned. This time she carefully marks her way: she looks for a good elementary discussion of deconstruction; she quotes from an introduction to literary theory that she has tracked down; she thinks her way through the opening lines of *John* using the vocabulary she has now begun to master. This is what we would call "process writing," and Erin is indeed proceeding, for not only is she trying the ideas out but, unlike in a free-writing exercise, she is trying them out *on someone*. For Erin, plagued as she is with the kind of underconfidence that we see in so many of our bright graduate students, this, I think, makes all the difference. Like Rebecca, she too wrote a fine and theoretically-confident paper at the end of the semester.[5]

The Middle Way

I remain surprised and delighted by the tangible success of this exercise in the graduate class; there truly were no "failed" correspondences. I should add as a final point, however, that some of the graduate teaching fellows in the class tried out a version of this assignment in their first-year composition classes in the semester following the graduate course and most of them were profoundly disappointed in the results. I think the answer for why this was the case lies in an eloquent summary written by one of the graduate students at the end of English 360. Commenting on her experience of encountering the Biblical text as literature, the student wrote:

> I would say that through my own exploration, I've come to understand the book itself as a method of literary exploration of the fundamental reality of life. Although there are repetitions of stories, familiarities of themes, although there is a beginning and an end, both as a cohesive text and as a story, I'm left with the feeling that the middle ground remains to be known, and that every hypothesis we concoct is in some ways our own personal mapping expedition, and not an Answer.

Although the student is ostensibly describing her experience of the Bible, her words might well apply to the letter-writing assignment. The correspondence assignment will only work if students are prepared to surrender themselves to the "middle ground." In my own experience, undergraduates, most of whom are still very nervous about the possibility that "every hypothesis we concoct is in some ways our own personal mapping expedition," are simply not quite ready for the risks—personal and intellectual—they must be willing to take if this assignment is truly to work. I'm grateful to the students in English 360, who were willing to spend some time exploring the middle way; I know that I have never been as gratified by student writing as I was in that class.

Notes

I am grateful to the careful and insightful readings the contributors of this volume—valued colleagues all—gave to early drafts of this paper. I want especially to acknowledge, however, the students of English 360 from the Spring of 1998 who gave me so much more than the insights contained in this paper.

1. I did reassure them that I would certainly tell them if they were completely off-track, but otherwise, I wanted the conversation to be theirs and theirs alone. I didn't want them to write—as they do with their papers—with me as their imagined audience.

2. Of course, as luck would have it, I originally had 17 people in the class. I decided, then, to have one group of three. We were just underway when one of the members of the class dropped out; she was not, unfortunately, part of the group of three. Rather than disturb things too much—I was really happy with the pairs and the group— I decided, with his sanction, to become the correspondence partner of the person who had lost his partner. We were, it turned out, a good pair, and I think it made a huge, though unmeasureable, difference to the class that I was also involved in a correspondence and not only an eavesdropper.

Mid-way through the semester, a continuing education student with unmanageable full-time work demands also dropped the course. At that point, I was unwilling to forfeit my own correspondence for I had recognized its worth both to the partnership but also to the class as a whole, so I broke up the threesome and reassigned one of its members to the student who had been left without a partner. I therefore had the fortuitous opportunity to see, quite by accident, how variations of this exercise might work, in particular, the possibility of conducting a correspondence in larger groups, and the value of switching partners mid-stream. Although one of the members of the threesome did not concur, I actually thought that the larger group worked remarkably well. This is a variation I will probably experiment with in future classes. I did *not* think it was advantageous to switch partners mid-stream, however; it was clear to me at the end of the course that the students needed the whole semester to achieve the kind of epistolary relationships that were most valuable.

3. While I can imagine ways in which a professor's responses to student writing might encourage the growth I saw in both Steve and Jason, I think the transformation is actually helped along by the relatively small amount of professorial intrusion. Yes, I was reading their letters; yes, I was going to issue a grade at the end of the course—but there were measurable ways in which they both seemed to have forgotten that. For instance, at the beginning of the correspondence they were urging me—in handwritten pleas at the ends of their letters—to weigh in on the authority/interpretation/ideology issue (which I did in a brief e-mail and then deflected by giving them copies of an essay by Steven Mailloux called "Interpretation"). However, about five weeks into the course they were both consistently forgetting to bring *my* copy of their letters to class (although they never forgot to bring a copy for their partner). Indeed, this "forgetting" was not unique to Steve and Jason; lots of people throughout the semester were forgetting to bring in the professor-copies of their letters. Other markers of my absence included pairs alluding to conversations they had had outside of class without providing any context for me; many of them became much more familiar with each other, even using nicknames and talking much more about their personal lives; in one memorable example, a

pair that had occasionally represented curse words à la comic books—"f*&@"—as if anxious that I might be shocked or disapproving, started writing them out in full, and with abandon.

4. And that paper, inherently more complex than this one, would doubtless reflect at length on the role that gender plays in the graduate classroom.

5. In personal conversations after the fact, both women said (not surprisingly) that they were not consciously aware of the way in which the letters were operating as a kind of "talking cure" for them.

9

Letters and Critical Conversation
in a Graduate Seminar

Mary Jane Dickerson

At the first meeting of a spring 1997 graduate seminar "Faulkner and Morrison: The Color Line in the 20th Century," its syllabus still in progress, I asked students to consider what kinds of written and oral assignments they thought best suited for our semester's work together. Nicole immediately spoke up to ask if, instead of the usual individual presentations, we might organize small groups for scheduled panel presentations around one topic. Her interesting suggestion for collaborative work led to my complete overhaul of the conventional graduate seminar format with its emphasis on individual assignments (for example, reading journal, individual oral presentation, major research essay) toward a final portfolio reflecting the multifaceted nature of students' oral and written work. At the second seminar meeting, we formed three groups with three members (and one with four) to facilitate in-class discussions, to organize presentation panels, and to share written work. With our one auditor, we had six students who were African American and Asian American, with the other eight European and European American—an opportunity for shaping a dynamic learning community for considering literary representations of race in America and their implications for each of us.

By far the single most important syllabus modification stemmed from my decision to change the usual weekly journal assignment, a change that came out of students' desire for ways to communicate their ideas with each other. Rather than require students to keep a reading-response journal meant primarily to focus class discussion and for me to collect and read periodically, we agreed students should direct their reading responses each week (at this point, not specifically called "a letter") to their small group members and circulate them. Since these students were already interested in reading Faulkner and Morrison, in discussing the course topics and in listening to what others had to say, it didn't appear necessary to impose rigid rules governing the journal letters.

What seemed most beneficial for such small group correspondence was to give students the freedom to speculate, raise questions, even to digress in productive ways as they read texts that challenged our notions of individual and collective identities and, most of all, to engage in dialogue with others. This ongoing assignment led naturally to the notion of a final portfolio instead of the conventional critical essay that ordinarily concludes a graduate seminar; these would be assembled in creative ways to show reading, critical thinking, collaborating and writing as a developing experience. What follows is a description of how this journal-letter writing process, as it evolved out of individual and group needs over a semester, enriched panel presentations, class discussion, and the contents of students' final portfolios to make them into stories of learning.[1]

Every week, each student wrote one response to the reading, providing copies for the other three group members; each then responded to the others' pieces. Immediately and without prompting, most group members began addressing their responses to each other by either "Dear Megan" or, at least, by name—"Jaime" or "Wandra." Students might sometimes respond to group members individually, at other times collectively in a single letter with paragraphs specifically directed to individuals. Soon, communication by "journal letter" extended to intra-group e-mail as students set up discussion meetings with topics and questions to address (sometimes directing these informational discussion messages to me so that I might participate if my schedule permitted: see the e-mail below).

After the second week, students were responsible for exchanging these "journal letters" between class meetings, and we set aside the last twenty minutes of class time to discuss what had taken place and to add ideas as postscripts stimulated by the exchanges. This often concluded our time with a productive burst of energy—people with their heads close together as their comparative reading led them in different directions or a pair who had discovered a mutual interest: a contrast to what often turns into dead time at the end of a long day. As each group gave me copies of these epistolary conversations at appropriate one-to-two week intervals (theirs the decision and the schedule), I too responded to their ongoing observations and arguments with comments and questions of my own in brief end-letters and marginal commentary, thus contributing to the conversation as a participant-observer rather than evaluator only—a crucial result of the journal as letter. As loose as this weekly process sounds, it soon took on a life of its own.

Two things happened almost immediately: 1) the journal letters helped the groups organize and develop material for substantial panel presentations which, in turn, stimulated essay topics and other creative ideas for putting together a final portfolio with its own "cover letter"—another beneficial result of the assignment overhaul; 2) the letters offered opportunities for critical debate and discussion beyond boundaries of time and place; these conversations often transcended the journal letters circulated within the class, taking place through e-mail and even in cross-group letters as what happened in class stimulated further exchange similar to Megan's and Nicole's in an example described below. If one student recognized a shared concern or issue during class discussion, for example, another correspondence might take place as a single exchange or several over time as an extra conversation. It's as if the dialectic between Faulkner and Morrison on meanings of the "Color Line" in the twentieth century reflected itself in the ongoing dialogues promoted by the exchange of journal letters in the seminar, dialogues that took on a life of their own beyond the classroom. The end result was that many of the final portfolios reflected this multivocality of students in conversation with each other to provide an interesting echo of the polyphony characterizing Faulkner's and Morrison's rendering of their own fictional worlds. What follows are some examples of letters creating critical conversation in some of the productive ways enumerated above.

Journal Letters: Class Work

Here's Gray responding to Megan's journal letter about certain Faulkner and Morrison women characters whose worlds are circumscribed by their relationships with men. A lengthy and richly speculative piece, its significance lies primarily in the way Gray interrogates Megan's own speculations, an interrogation that pushes Megan's thinking toward even richer readings of these women characters and challenges Gray herself to think about their positions. An excerpt:

> Megan:
> Where do I start? I'm glad you got a chance to explore the links between Temple [Faulkner's *Sanctuary*] and Dorcas [Morrison's *Jazz*] . . . since we never quite got there during class discussion. I'm also glad you pulled in Wild [*Jazz*]. Wild does seem to be outside the traditional female boundaries, in a place of her own. She's the one the men are afraid of, yet drawn to. . . . You're absolutely right, female sexuality in these texts is "tangled up with objectification, power and control." You didn't want to go into the gaze, but I'd say that's a very integral part of it. . . . Wild is a bit of a paradox, though; I can't argue with your statement that she is objectified, and yet I feel as though, by remaining on the periphery of the gaze of men, she's still living on her own terms.

What's interesting here is the way Gray acknowledges the limitations of class time and the value of having discussions beyond those limitations about topics of mutual concern. Gray also shows her attention to Megan's reading by quoting from Megan's journal letter and incorporating Megan's language into the response, and she does so in order to point out her own modification—to narrate her own story of Wild's characterization in contrast to that of Dorcas and Temple.

Gray ends her journal letter to Megan by validating and expanding Megan's own analysis, further interrogating their, by this time, mutual reading experience of these female characters in Faulkner and Morrison:

> The respective sexuality of Dorcas and Temple is cre-
> ated by the fact that they are the objects of the gaze
> of men. Wild seems to escape by virtue of not allow-
> ing herself to be the object of the gaze. I noted in
> my last class journal that there is a section in *Sanc-
> tuary* when Temple remembers an incident with some
> classmates (p. 151): "The worst one of all said boys
> thought all girls were ugly except when they were
> dressed. She said the Snake had been seeing Eve for
> several days and never noticed her until Adam made
> her put on a fig leaf." So is Wild outside of the gaze
> and objectification because she doesn't wear cloth-
> ing? It is stated in *Jazz* that Dorcas and Felice both
> "know that a badly dressed body is nobody at all"
> (p. 65). So what does that make an undressed body?
>
>   Gray

Megan's response to Gray's question is to explore the relationships between women's bodies and houses in these novels as she reads yet another novel, Faulkner's *Absalom, Absalom!:*

> Many of Faulkner and Morrison's stories are framed by
> literal houses. . . . In subtle ways, the stories are
> also framed by physical bodies. . . . Characters of-
> ten share characteristics with their dwellings. Ger-
> aldine in *The Bluest Eye* has no hold with "funk" and
> neither does her home; in *Sancturary,* Ruby's harsh
> life is exemplified by her protecting the baby from
> rats; Wild inhabits the woods in *Jazz;* Polly Breed-
> love is only happy tending house for her white mis-
> tress; and finally, Miss Rosa's body is decaying as a
> virgin spinster locked up in a stale house.

From their conversation, Megan expands her own view of the functions of women's bodies as she continues to reflect on other women characters throughout these novels.

As group work got underway for the presentations in the second half of the semester, other letters such as the e-mail below show how involved students were in their presentation preparation. On occasion, I found myself with these groups, especially those whose topics and texts were most important to me and my ongoing work with Faulkner and Morrison, just to be part of what was going on as they read and wrote to me and each other.

Here's what Tony wrote to his Faulkner/Morrison group as they were working on their panel presentation on Faulkner's *Absalom, Absalom!* and Morrison's *Beloved:*

```
Hi All,
     Beth and I just met with Mary Jane and we decided
to make the initial foray into both scheduling a
meeting time and starting the discussion. So, how
does 9:00 A.M. on Tuesday sound to everyone? The meet-
ing should last about an hour, so let us know if that
time is good or any alternate time(s).
     As for subject matter, we three were interested
in the issues surrounding gender and, by extension,
sexuality in the texts. In other words, how is gen-
der constructed and/or articulated through char-
acters and relationships? Also, what about sexual-
ity? What are some of the complications that arise
out of heterocentrist/sexist texts and what are the
implications?
     I have this funny feeling that all of us will ap-
proach the varying constructions of gender and sexu-
ality in Beloved and Absalom, Absalom! in different
ways (including how "race," class, etc. impact such
constructions); and this seems to be what we're going
for. So, put on the gloves and come out swinging —
epistemologically speaking, of course.
                                              Tony
```

As Tony requested, the group met, with his thoughtful questions, developed from small group discussion, providing the framework for a rich conversation that took us into areas later reflected in the group's lively presentation to the class and a subsequent flurry of journal letters, some of which got incorporated in their final portfolios.

Journal Letters: Portfolios

In a revised plan for his final portfolio, Tony wrote that he wanted to include five of his most engaged journal letters: "I've had wonderful theoretical conversations with Kathryn and Beth, . . . I will include my interactions with them." In that way, their conversations through journal letter added to what, for some like Tony, became almost collaborative portfolios, in that their portfolios reflected an interactive dialogue.

In her portfolio proposal, Beth, one of Tony's cohorts, wrote:

> As I review the available critical works in this field
> [landscape and nature imagery in Faulkner and Mor-
> rison's texts], I will continue a written conversa-
> tion with Kathryn and Tony which began with the first
> journal entry for the course. Although our interests
> aren't the same, we've discovered intriguing inter-
> sections and overlappings of our ideas, and their in-
> put so far has been fascinating and very helpful in
> suggesting new areas of development. The journal en-
> tries included in my portfolio will reveal my ideas
> and questions about the texts and the dialogue from
> Kathryn and Tony as well.

Such out-of-class discussions through letters to each other allowed me to observe these students in the process of thinking through the tangled issues of gender, race and the uses of history these texts demanded of us. Whether or not journal letter exchanges always actually made it into all the portfolios, these letter discussions shaped the critical conversation reflected in portfolio content. Often, I felt as if I were invited behind the scenes of the seminar itself, espe-cially when I saw my own words circulating among theirs as we tried out our ideas in this respectful and open forum.

One of the stipulations for the portfolio and its freedom of genres was that students were to bring their knowledge of the Faulkner/Morrison criticism to bear on whatever they eventually chose to include. Since students' letter con-versations often drew on their secondary readings and since they found creative ways to use that reading in their letters, some ventured into other genres when they didn't feel absolutely compelled to focus their major writing projects pri-marily on criticism. It was as if their critical conversations through the journal letter pieces freed them to try other writing experiences. Here's what Nicole wrote in her portfolio proposal:

> An autocritical essay . . . that looks at the uses of
> ambiguity that both authors seem to employ and its
> ramifications for us as readers. I'm not really inter-
> ested in writing a critical research essay because too
> much of the research often seems to get in the way of
> *my own* understanding. And as an eventual scholar I
> feel that I really need to work on articulating my own
> perspective without relying on established critics/
> writers for validation. I am interested in pursuing
> what Nancy Welch has referred to as "other stories,"
> looking for the tensions/connections that *I* see in
> my reading, trying to move away from locating knowl-
> edge along the Oedipal axis.

At other places in her proposal, Nicole stipulated that in one portfolio section she planned to include her dialogues with different people in the class—she is one who had carried on conversations across the organized class groups, as a later look at Megan's portfolio will illustrate.

Kathryn, another of Tony and Beth's cohorts, also mentions, like Nicole above, her need to extend the nature of her critical investigations, as she describes here in her revised portfolio proposal:

```
From my readings of Morrison and Faulkner, I have a
more developed idea of how I view "race" miscegena-
tion so I want to try my hand at exploring those in a
fictional framework as well. I'm particularly inter-
ested in Faulkner's ever varied narrative techniques
as well as Morrison's view(s) of history and lineage
(and by saying that, I must also state that I find each
concept fascinating in the other as well). This story
will investigate the "color line" as it applies to
Chinese Americans that live within an American cul-
ture that is apart, similar to blacks during and af-
ter slavery, from the "home" country yet still strug-
gling to create a dispensation for themselves, like
Thomas Sutpen, in a dynamic South.
```

Kathryn also mentioned, in her plans for the portfolio "Cover Letter," that this narrative project is a revision of a story she had attempted in my colleague Nancy Welch's class, Studies in Composition and Rhetoric. Both Nicole and Kathryn saw connections between their collaborative reading experiences in the Faulkner/Morrison seminar and expanded possibilities for their writing projects stemming from Nancy Welch's notion of those "other stories" lurking within what we read and what we write—what's always missing. Reading Faulkner and Morrison narratives is an exercise in straining to listen to all those "other stories" that keep slipping into the fissures of narrative structures.

In the same small group, Nicole and Kathryn were able to continue, through journal letters and classroom dialogue, their own exercises in listening to those "other stories." In *Getting Restless,* Nancy Welch's central concern is with revision in composition, but I think her ideas apply to an ongoing revision students undergo when they meet the dissonance produced in Morrison and Faulkner's fictions and when they articulate their own dissonant responses. Welch even describes a reading experience as part of that revisionary process when she writes "That moment of reading worked to disrupt continuity, development, and unfolding; it raised the discomforting but revisionary questions: *What am I becoming?* and *What else might I become?*" (31). Kathryn's portfolio finally included both her narrative "Miscegenation" about suppressed family stories and a related critical essay "Why 2 + 2 (can no longer) = 4: Undoing American Racism, Undermining Hierarchies." These pieces resonate with the journal-letter conversations Kathryn had carried on with Tony, Beth and

Nicole as they worked out issues of self and other in Faulkner and Morrison and confronted the significance of these things in their own lives.

Of all the proposed uses of the semester journal-letter exchanges in the portfolio-writing projects, Megan found one of the most innovative and productive, as she takes up Morrison's challenge in *Playing In The Dark,* to draw a "critical geography" of reading whiteness and blackness. Megan writes that "this notion of reading both texts [black and white] in an effort to understand the dialogue *between* is precisely the kind of fluid conversation that English 320 has created in reading William Faulkner and Toni Morrison together." She proceeds to interweave a series of what she calls "annotated journal entries" with significant letters from others that stimulated further responses from her and finally resulted in one formal essay and an afterword. Here is one example of dialogue at work as Megan reflects on a fruitful exchange with Nicole, from another group:

> Nicole and I were on similar terrain in terms of the
> role of the gaze that week. She responded:
>
> > Megan — This idea of the "gaze" is an interest-
> > ing one especially since Temple's rape is "wit-
> > nessed" by two people who cannot/do not have ac-
> > cess to this gaze — the idiot . . . Tommy, and the
> > old blind man (not to mention the rats). Maybe
> > it's possible that Faulkner is commenting on the
> > power of the gaze or our desire/penchant for as-
> > signing power to the gaze (seeing is believing).
>
> Nicole introduces the idea of "power" which I had not
> articulated in my own reading. I think we do assign
> power to the looker, to the gaze, rather than the
> "looked at." Is there power in being the object of a
> masculine gaze? . . . We discussed these issues in
> class, and I'll admit that women can and often do
> subvert the role of object by using desire as a form
> of power. However . . .

Other letters from members of her group—Jaime, Wandra, and Gray, including the earlier example as well as the exchange with Nicole above—show how important their correspondence had become to her semester's reading and writing experience: a dialogue among texts by the white male writer and the black female writer; a dialogue of journal letters among Megan and her cohorts in which they pose questions to each other; all are dialogues that finally constitute the "fluid conversation" of the seminar as it is reflected in Megan's portfolio. It's almost inevitable after the discussion Megan carries on with others about women's bodies, the male gaze, and bodies and houses that she follows her reconstruction of that interactive dialogue in her portfolio with an essay

"'But that girl': Looking at Rape in *Go Down, Moses* and *The Bluest Eye*." By positioning the essay in such relationship to the sequence of journal letters, Megan demonstrates how the essay came into being.

In the introductory words to her portfolio, Megan puts it this way: "My map does not offer a permanent record of place or destination, but rather a landscape of possibilities." Such a portfolio as Megan's, with its interactive/dialogic sequence of journal writings that represent collaborative work and lead toward significant critical thinking and writing, shows what distinguished the best of the seminar's portfolios. At times, to be sure, we had logistical problems of who was to read what and when, and I had to consider how to think and respond in appropriate holistic ways when authorship becomes problematic in the give and take of complex conversations, but these problems always paled in the richness of what began to take place beyond the seminar boundaries. And finally, my response letter to students' portfolios also reflected altered relationships between students and teacher because those boundaries had also shifted in the give and take of ideas and readings during the seminar—a pleasing result for me.

Here's one thing I wrote to Beth: "I appreciated the way your particular selections of journal letters gave a sense of your thinking, especially in its inflections from those you were in dialogue with throughout the semester." By the time I read her portfolio, I could almost hear Tony, Nicole and Kathryn's voices as they took issue, mediated, questioned, and agreed with Beth's evolving discussion of the homoeroticism slipping through spaces in Faulkner and Morrison narratives. In commenting on Megan's annotated letter journals essay and how it contextualizes the essay on rape, I recognized that the dialogic process was still at work: "As you can see, I even started interacting with your presentation of your reading experience as if we were still in the midst of it because reading this section of the portfolio set me to thinking again." I also found myself urging that they continue work on many of these pieces of writing because they had taken on a life beyond the boundaries of the seminar. To Kathryn on her memoir piece "Miscegenation": "I am so glad you included this memoir that does address in powerful ways what Faulkner and Morrison struggle toward expressing. Your work shows how much yet remains to be written about the effects of the many premutations of the color line in our complex society and its role in the global." Kathryn's narrative worked to further complicate Faulkner and Morrison's own stories of race and gender in American society.

Further Correspondence

Dear Mary Jane,

I really like what you did with your graduate seminar because it seems to bring *into* your class the interaction with peers that was for me the best part of graduate school. Both my master's and my doctoratal study were at schools where students set up for

```
themselves  a  collaborative  atmosphere,  even  though
the  collaboration  hardly  ever  developed  because  of
anything  structured  into  the  course.  It  would  have
been  interesting  to  see  what  might  have  happened  if
it  had  been  a  part  of  what  we  were  asked  to  do.
```
Rebecca Wall

At the conclusion of a panel on letters in the classroom at the 1999 4C's in Atlanta [the panel moderator asked for letter responses from the audience], I received a number of letters from people like Rebecca Wall who added their own perspective to the paper I had presented, a shortened version of this essay. Four responses were from former students, either teachers themselves or doctoral students preparing to teach. Two—Beth and Megan—had been members of the Faulkner-Morrison seminar and found their work part of the discussion.

Here's what Megan wrote about seeing her words on an overhead transparency:

```
.  .  .  seeing  my  own  letters  on  the  OHP  and  hearing
you talk  about  the  Morrison/Faulkner  seminar  reminded
me  how  powerful  that  class  was  for  all  of  us  in  it.
And  the  letter  writing  opportunity  that  you  gave  us
was  a  huge  component  in  making  it  so.  That  class  was
instrumental  for  me  in  so  many  ways  —  I  felt  like  an
independent  scholar  for  one  of  the  first  times  ever.  I
also  felt  that  I  established  a  true  intellectual  and
emotional  community  (that  I  still  feel  today)  with
those  with  whom  I  exchanged  letters  —  Nicole,  Jamie,
Wandra
```

What I would add to Megan's observation is that the seminar's assignments and format gave students a space to invent themselves, to "become" scholars who shaped themselves into a community. Perhaps it's this possibility for self-invention through reading and writing that another former student, Karen, was referring to when she observed that "graduate students are another category of 'at risk' writers, who really need the P. S. (personal stuff) that spaces in letters provide."

Notes

1. I would like to thank all of the students in my 1997 graduate seminar "Faulkner and Morrison: The Color Line in the 20th Century" for giving me permission to quote from their journals, e-mails, and final portfolios.

Work Cited

Welch, N. 1997. *Getting Restless: Rethinking Revision in Writing Instruction.* Portsmouth, NH: Boynton/Cook.

10

"Taking Care"

Training Tutors Through Letters

Jean Kiedaisch

```
April 27
Dear Jean —

I like the letter exchange process because I enjoy re-
ceiving feedback on my sessions. Since it is informal
it's easier to pose questions or ask for suggestions.
. . . The other thing I like about letters is the per-
sonal aspect. I have only a handful of classes (mostly
Women's Studies) where I can develop a conversation
with a professor outside of class. And essentially
that's what I consider the letter exchange — an on-
going conversation. So thanks for the talk!

                                        Take Care,
                                        Leilani
```

In her final letter, written at the end of a year of tutoring, Leilani comments on the letter exchange that is at the heart of the training for peer tutors at the University of Vermont Writing Center. What she says she found, a safe place to ask questions or seek advice and a personal relationship created and maintained by conversation, is what I intended in exchanging letters with peer writing tutors. I reasoned that even though I invite tutors to come talk in person, the reflection involved in writing letters would help deepen our conversation. And as expected, at year's end, I knew fifteen tutors well, trusted what happened in their sessions, and had an ongoing stake in their growth as tutors and as people. With a sense of satisfaction, I read a set of final letters like Leilani's.

It was only later, when beginning work on this chapter, that I re-read, one tutor's letters at a time and looked at a year's worth of correspondence. In doing so, I saw how much more was going on than I had at first realized. In particular,

I noticed how each writer had used the letter exchange to articulate an identity as a tutor. My role in the letter exchange had been to affirm and extend the tutors' thinking about the assumptions, beliefs, style, and strategies that went into making up that identity.

This process of articulation can be seen unfolding in the letters of tutor Brendan Lucey. When we exchanged letters, Brendan was a junior at the University of Vermont, a biology major with history and English minors. An excellent student, he was a finalist for a Truman Scholarship, an intellectually curious and thoughtful person with a quirky sense of humor. He impressed me most by not being overly impressed with himself and his achievements—he thought he still had more to learn. He was interested in writers as individuals and in their particular needs, having grasped why Stephen North (1984) says: "our job is to produce better writers, not better writing."

Brendan tended to be quiet in class, making me appreciate his letters even more as a way to find out what he was thinking. And in these letters he was articulate, honest, and above all reflective. Re-reading Brendan's letters, I was struck by the implicit questions he seemed to be asking and answering. These questions organize the following look at how Brendan articulates a tutor identity.

Why Do I Want to Be a Writing Tutor?

This question, which could also be formulated as "how invested am I in this process of becoming a writing tutor?" is a natural starting point. Tutoring is hard work; where does the motivation to do it well come from? In his first letter of the semester, Brendan begins thinking on paper about what, in addition to the fact that it was flattering to be recommended, has brought him to tutoring. The whole idea, he says, "excited me":

```
September 10
Dear Jean,

    . . . I love to write and welcome the chance to help
others, if I can, with their writing. . . . An hour
does not grant much time to work on a piece of writ-
ing; hopefully, a process will be established during
the tutoring session to allow the student to complete
the paper independently. The student would then, ide-
ally, possess the skills to write without the same
problems or concerns.
```

When I read Brendan's letter, I found much I wanted to affirm. I was delighted that he began with a desire to help other writers—surely there's no better place to start. And I was pleased that he saw an hour-long session as only initiating the revision process. But I did want him to think more about whether in one session the writer would acquire all "the skills to write without the same problems or concerns" she'd had when she came to the writing center or whether writers really outgrow the need to hear from readers. And so I wrote back, in part,

Dear Brendan,

[you mention] establishing a process . . . that allows the student to complete the paper independently,
which I agree with (though I think you have to urge
the student to take careful notes during the session
and check to see what s/he is planning to do in revising). . . . I know in the Learning Co-op we're always talking about creating "independent learners"
but . . . as a writer I never plan to get to the place
where I no longer want another reader to offer me his
or her response. . . . What's your experience as a
writer?

I wanted Brendan to think about a possible distinction between the indepen-
dence that allows a writer to continue what was begun in a session and "independent" meaning not needing readers. Perhaps here Brendan's writerly identity could inform his tutor identity.

Brendan has another reason for wanting to be a tutor:

My personal experience at the Writing Center led me
to tutoring. [He explains that he was working on a
collaborative piece with a partner who suggested
they come; the tutor hadn't read their author, lim-
iting what they could do in the session.] The hour
did not lead to any productive, constructive changes
in the paper and I felt the time wasted. . . . I decided to tutor writing because I wanted to try to
provide students who came to my sessions with a better experience than I had.

I applauded Brendan's not giving up on the Writing Center because of one
disappointing session. It said a lot about him: he could see the potential of the
peer tutoring relationship even when his own session fell short of the ideal. And
he was surely right about the importance to the session of the text about which
he and his partner were writing. When it was left out of the discussion, the session was limited. This led me to ask: "Could you have shown the tutor key passages you were working with that he could have read on the spot? I guess I'm
asking if you can revisit that session to think about how a tutor might have/
could have made that a worthwhile session."

I wanted Brendan to grapple with the problem that tutors can never be in a
position to have read everything a student might be writing about, and with the
implications that has for sessions. I wish I had a reply from Brendan, but truth-
fully, I often didn't get one. Since our class met once a week and at each class
I returned a letter and got a new one, tutors had to either remember my questions for a week or re-read my letter in order to respond, something they only
occasionally did.

What Do I Know or Need to Learn?
What Is It Ok Not to Know?

In our center, tutors begin having sessions in the fourth week of their training, a fact that produces both excitement and anxiety. Most tutors ask themselves whether they know enough to help another student writer; the question as they most often articulate it is "What if I read the paper and have nothing to say?" I wanted to show them that they know how to offer a reader's (as opposed to a teacher's) response. And so for the third week's class the tutors were asked to write about the agenda they might set for a session over each of three personal essays from first-year students. Personal essays were chosen because in the early weeks of tutoring, these were the papers first-year composition students were likely to be bringing to the writing center. Brendan is different from some of the other tutors in having a lot to say and feeling confident about his responses. For each of the three papers, he offers a half-page list of responses and questions for the writer. For example,

```
September 17
Dear Jean,

    I greatly enjoyed the sample essays provided in
the last class. Each had a distinctive flavor that
drew me into the story. . . . The last essay is guilty
of a problem I have encountered many times myself:
the author attempts to include everything into his
paper. This problem creates a lack of clarity and de-
tail that would otherwise make the paper very strong.
Also, the organization of the paper needs work. . . .
He tries to start in the middle of the action, but
has difficulty making the time transition back to the
story's start.
```

I shared with Brendan my own reading of each of the three personal essays, sometimes agreeing with his reading, sometimes adding to it, as I did with his response to the essay he comments on above:

```
Dear Brendan,

    One thing the Japan paper brings up for me is this:
sometimes a paper that would be a weak final draft is
in fact an excellent first draft. I agree with every-
thing you say about the paper, but you could begin a
session with this writer by complimenting him on how
many ideas he was able to get down on paper where he
could look at them — that makes choosing what to keep
or where to focus easier. And it means you as tutor
can respond as a reader — "Here are some of the places
I was most intrigued or wanted to know more."
```

I saw an opportunity to push Brendan's thinking about different goals for different drafts of a paper's development. Here again I don't have a response to my letter, because of how the exchange was structured—we were on to a new week and a new letter. But two weeks later he shows that he has enough sense of writing as process to know when not to move too quickly to a first draft:

> October 8
> Dear Jean,
>
> I had several interesting tutoring sessions this week. First, a young man wanted help in generating and developing an idea for an editorial. . . . His beginning topic was on UVM and alcohol, but after talking with him for several minutes he realized that he was more concerned about partying in particular, than alcohol consumption specifically. . . . We really found out what he wanted to do when he spontaneously started talking about his experiences with partying, and how he tried to find a balance between academics and having fun. He thinks that the process of finding such a balance is an important part of maturing, learning to live on one's own, and that this is an important reason for attending university.

Obviously, what this young man needed most was the opportunity to talk with a person interested in his ideas, and Brendan knew this was the appropriate way to spend their hour. I could only reply: "Wow! I'm impressed with that session . . ., both with what you did and with what he did. . . . To end up with his own idea of why we come to college is valuable indeed!"

But while Brendan knows that he has a lot to say about student papers and topics, he, like almost every other tutor in the class, is not so confident about his grasp of the rules of "grammar":

> October 1
> Dear Jean,
>
> I felt apprehensive about becoming a writing tutor when I learned Nancy had recommended me because I did not believe I could help students edit papers. Even though my grammar skills have not improved over the summer, I now feel I will become a quality writing tutor. I realized that I actually know more grammar than I think. . . . Nevertheless, I have to refresh my grammar knowledge as I did this week with Hacker [a brief handbook all the tutors used].

In responding to this concern, I wanted to reassure Brendan that he certainly didn't need to take on the task of knowing all the rules in a handbook:

"Many tutors are just like you: they use their ears, not rules when editing. And that will get you a long way. For what you can't hear, i.e., for what needs to be looked up, you can model for your tutees how to use a handbook." Tutors do model the practices of good writers for the student writers with whom they work.

For Brendan, it was not so easy to make "model writer" part of his identity, perhaps because of his notion that the student should be in the position of power. Later in the semester, he worked with a student struggling to write an introduction to a history paper. He showed her an introduction that he himself had just written and talked with her about what he'd been trying to do in his introduction. He said in his letter, "I'm not sure if this was the best thing to do. It may have been more productive to have her write something, but I thought that seeing a concrete example would be useful." I thought what Brendan did was excellent: "you're relating as peers, both working on your writing. And concrete is always a better starting place than abstract."

Through our letter exchange, Brendan came to the conclusion that there wasn't a lot of "information" he needed to know. Rather, he needed to adopt a particular stance with student writers: attentive, interested reader and writer willing to share his own practices—and struggles.

How was I Taught to Write and Respond to Others' Writing?

Inevitably, as tutors begin tutoring, they think back to writing teachers they have had, the kind of instruction they received, the way that responding to others' writing was taught. The previous year Brendan had been enrolled in a writing class with Nancy Welch, who was also the person who had recommended him as a writing tutor. Brendan considers its impact:

```
September 24
Dear Jean,

    . . . The course completely changed my attitudes to-
ward my writing and the revision process. [Before the
course] I looked at revision purely as an exercise in
working out the kinks of spelling, capitalization,
punctuation, sentence structure, and the repairing
of clumsy, unclear passages. . . . My writing looked
good, and probably sounded all right, but it lacked
thick, compelling substance. I never examined my
first drafts for new material, new directions, in-
stead placing my faith in the original ideas. . . .
In English 50, I watched Nancy find single sentences
that fit into the paper, but seemed to leave something
out. They contained meanings deeper than the ones I
originally fleshed out. By reflecting on these sen-
tences, I might change my entire paper. . . .
```

Reading this letter, I could tell Brendan was discovering that as a tutor, he wanted to work with student writers on revision in the same way Nancy had worked with him. Furthermore, he realized he had gained some strategies he could make use of in his sessions and perhaps teach other writers. I responded:

```
September 27
Dear Brendan,
    I'm happy to hear that taking a class with Nancy
gave you a whole new concept of revision. . . . In
your letter, as you talked about how you'd like to
go about tutoring, I inferred that you want to use
Nancy's techniques. . . . For the next class, . . .
we'd like to have those of you who've had Nancy in
class describe a few of her techniques, as a way to
show what kind of practice grows out of her theory
[as they'd encountered it in Getting Restless (1997),
one of the texts for the course].
```

Not only can Brendan teach the student writers with whom he works some useful strategies, he can share them with his fellow tutors.

In his writing class Brendan had also been asked to respond to the writing of his classmates. When in the tutor-training class we read Kenneth Bruffee's "Peer Tutoring and the 'Conversation of Mankind'" (1984),in which he makes a case for peer tutoring as "conversation within a community of knowledgeable peers," Brendan's response told me that he had practiced working collaboratively:

```
September 10
Dear Jean,
    I agree most whole-heartedly with the assertion
that collaboration should be the primary vehicle
through which the student and tutor interact. Collab-
oration leads to discussion and the sorting of ideas.
A solid, well-thought out, well-written paper will
result from clearly understanding what needs saying;
such understanding can best be obtained through con-
versation. . . . The most difficult part of tutoring
I foresee is simply starting the dialogue, the col-
laboration, that will progress the student's writing
and my own.
```

As good as Brendan feels about using collaborative practices in the writing center, in an in-class writing that same week, he said he was "a little concerned" about showing his writing to others. I responded that he'd be "in a good position to understand how [his] tutees are feeling when they come in for a session." I wanted to let him know that the sense of responsibility for the learning and also for the well-being of student writers never goes away. I wrote that "As a tutor [myself, in conferences with my tutors over their personal essays], I felt the way you may feel going into your first session—wondering if what I have to say will help you."

How Do I Position Myself with Student Writers?

Midway through the semester, we read Harvey Kail and John Trimbur's essay "The Politics of Peer Tutoring" (1987), in which the authors compare the curriculum-based model vs. the writing center model of tutoring. In the former, the tutor becomes a "little teacher" and retains the authority implied by that term, whereas in the latter, tutor and student writer relate as peers. Whether to position himself as authority or peer is a question Brendan never expresses in those terms. Still, he seems to grapple with its implications. For example, while he is excited at the possibility that he might help student writers find ways to revise, he also realizes an inherent danger:

```
September 24
Dear Jean,
    Tutoring presents the possibility for both a dan-
gerous and rewarding experience for me. It will be
dangerous if I try to steer students into directions
I think their papers should head. They might not see
or feel the connection and won't be able to write a
fulfilling paper. Conversely, if I can delicately
feel out where a student seems to want to go, I could
point out sentences I believe need exploration to
fully examine that direction. Laying the latter foun-
dation for students' papers will be much more reward-
ing for them because it will be their work, their hon-
esty, and their ideas in the paper.
```

Because the tutors are all such experienced writers, there *is* the danger they'll see (and recommend) what they would do with a given paper. Brendan seems to recognize two reasons why that wouldn't work: one, the student writer probably couldn't make very effective use of or have much investment in someone else's ideas and two, the student would miss the opportunity to fully examine his or her chosen direction.

In the hypothetical cases Brendan thinks about above, he has a choice between being an authority, explaining possible directions for the paper, or a peer, "delicately feel[ing] out where a student seems to want to go." However, in other situations, the role of peer is the only possibility. For example, Brendan is asked to tutor a student who is writing a paper analyzing a poem:

```
October 8
Dear Jean,

     I have always considered myself terrible at po-
etry, either writing about it or critically analyzing
it, and I told [the student writer] exactly that. We
bounced ideas back and forth about the poem and its
meaning to us, and tried to reach a consensus. He pro-
vided most of the direction here, with myself simply
giving suggestions about how I interpreted the poem.
Often, he would take an idea of mine as a starting
point that helped him develop a cohesive thesis about
the poem.
```

Brendan's letter gives me an opportunity to both point out and encourage his chosen role: "Interestingly, when you began the session by saying you were 'terrible at poetry,' you really set it up as a *peer* discussion—you were saying you didn't know any more about poetry than he did (hopefully less, since he was taking a class on it)."

In this case, Brendan very naturally assumed the role of peer. But what will he do when he clearly knows more about the subject than the student writer? Such was the case when a student brought in an American history paper:

```
October 29
Dear Jean,

     . . . By answering the question of why was Jef-
ferson inconsistent in his support of emancipation
and aristocracy, the student could fix the majority
of the problems in this paper. I am a history minor
and I was able to help her somewhat. I thought that
Jefferson removed emancipation from the Declaration
of Independence because it threatened to divide the
colonies. . . . The question of whether or not he was
a hypocrite is rather ambiguous. I recommended she
do a little more research and see what she could find,
and to talk with her professor to make sure this line
of thinking was on the right track.
```

Although Brendan is confident he can answer the professor's question and shares his own reading with the student, he passes the authority back to her by suggesting she do more research and talk to her professor. As he explains it, "If/when the student went to do more research, *they* would learn something, get more satisfaction, etc."

How Do I Read My Failures?

Inevitably for the tutors, some sessions go less well than they would like. They need to find a way to make room for imperfection in their tutor identities.

```
October 15
Dear Jean,

After the session, I was a little upset with myself
for not seeing the problems with the text clearer. I
believe I should have been more on the ball. . . .
When reading the paper, I was trying to simultane-
ously fix paper-wide organizational problems and edit.
Some sentences slipped through the cracks.

    As I revisit the session now, I believe the proper
course of action would have been to address one prob-
lem, then the other. Logically, the problem to attack
first is organization. . . . Yet, I failed to immedi-
ately realize some of the more subtle inconsisten-
cies. . . . Her original conclusion contained too
much information. I didn't completely understand how
to fix the conclusion until the final minutes of the
session.
```

Brendan ends the session "a little upset" with himself, but as he writes he is able to first analyze what got him into trouble. He then goes on to consider what he might have done differently, how complex the problems were, and how late in the session he figured some of them out. Having thought through all of that, he is ready to admit that tutors aren't perfect:

```
I have considered the possibility that I am attempt-
ing to take too much on my shoulders as a tutor. We
can't do everything in one hour. I don't believe
I should be faulted for simply failing to realize
how to connect two ideas, or how to re-structure a
paragraph.
```

In responding to this letter, it seemed most appropriate to simply reinforce the line of thinking Brendan was already taking:

```
October 21
Dear Brendan,
It's actually reassuring to get a letter like the one
you wrote this week. We all have sessions that in
hindsight we wish we had done somewhat differently.
I'd much rather have you do that kind of thinking back
over decisions you made and options you had than for
you to feel the need to defend what you did.
```

In my letter I also wanted to suggest another possible strategy to use when there's too much to do in a session, a strategy that can also help reinforce the student writer's learning:

> When you say "some sentences slipped through the cracks," I almost hear you saying that all errors need to be caught in a tutoring session or that all sentences that could be edited for style must be gotten to during the session. On the contrary, it's fine to do some with the student and then ask her to carry on at home.

All in all, I was pleased that the letter exchange helped Brendan recognize that tutors need to have realistic expectations for themselves, that these expectations should include the occasional disappointing session, and that "bad" sessions offer opportunities for learning.

What Theory Grows out of My Tutoring?

When tutors use letters to think further about their sessions, they begin developing their own tutoring theory, even though they may not use that term. Here are two examples of theory-building from Brendan's letters. First, his theory on editing for correctness:

> November 5
>
> Dear Jean,
>
> Sometimes I might ignore a professor's editing comments because I believe tutees should learn how to reconstruct their sentences and paragraphs, and spot grammatical errors. . . . As Meyer and Smith point out, it can be counter-productive for a student to simply correct the mistakes a professor indicates, then turn the paper back in. I would like for my tutees to spend time pondering over a mistake, and how to fix it, rather than to simply plug in the professor's written correction. Besides, students might not like a specific correction if it makes stylistic changes to their paper and may prefer to write it differently. If they can't make the correction on their own, they may feel like the paper is not truly theirs.

Brendan has figured out something some faculty members, in their thorough correcting of every error, have not: how ineffective it is to edit *for* a student writer. But not only is it ineffective, it also violates one of Brendan's most important goals, to, as he puts it, "make sure students keep their own style and voice." Brendan's theory on editing, one he most likely arrived at by writing about it, is based on both a pragmatic sense of what works and what doesn't and on an ethical stance.

A second theory began suggesting itself when we worked with all of the students in two business classes. We'd been asked to help them with style and editing, though the professor's description (to me) of his students' weaknesses included much more (e.g., "they over-quote because they're not confident in their understanding of the material"). Nevertheless, Brendan lamented the fact that "All those business students just wanted editing. They were very set on what they wanted to do. They'd give me the paper and just sit there." As a way of "dealing with them," Brendan began using editing as a way to get at larger issues. He and the student writer might fix, say, a punctuation problem, but then Brendan would let the sentence suggest a question that would force a broader discussion. This worked. The students, happy at getting to set the agenda for the session, were willing to answer Brendan's questions, and were thereby led quite naturally into deepening their thinking. Brendan was beginning to see new potential in sessions centered on editing.

Then came the midterm for the tutoring class. Tutors were asked to discuss in conference an interesting or problematic session, after making a copy of the paper they had tutored and reading it again to analyze the appropriateness of choices they had made for the session. As a tutor, Brendan likes to stay flexible and open to many possibilities ("I don't like to go in with too much of a plan"). He writes in his analysis of the American-history paper he was tutoring: "After reading through the paper once aloud, I could tell that she had great information but lacked an in-depth analysis." He decides, somewhat surprisingly, to work on editing to solve this problem and finds, still more surprisingly, that it is successful:

```
By editing the paper, we worked out the inconsisten-
cies in her thinking and tightened up the paper. I
thought that editing would be a prudent course of ac-
tion at this time because we could get a good grasp
of her argument by discussing how she was expressing
herself. Editing sentences and paragraphs helped her
re-see her thinking, as well as help her writing.
```

In our conference over this session, I pointed out that Brendan was going against conventional writing center wisdom, which would dictate working on ideas before working on editing, but that his explanation (basically, that it worked—that editing was an effective way to read) was compelling. Maybe he should work more on this idea and consider writing an article on revising through editing. (The third assignment in the tutor training course was to write an article for *The Dangling Modifier,* a newsletter by and for tutors, or *The Writing Lab Newsletter* or a talk for a peer tutoring conference. Brendan did in fact present his idea in a talk at the National Conference on Peer Tutoring in Writing in the fall of 1998.)

Several weeks later, Brendan's letter includes another example. The student had come in to work on a paper about Easy Cheese, a cheese that needs no refrigeration:

November 19
Dear Jean,

The student really wanted to work on finding places
in the paper she could elaborate on. . . . First, I
read the paper out loud. Then, we discussed the ideas
of the paper and tried to expand on them, or develop
new ones. We only thought of one or two, so I decided
to start editing. . . . Throughout the editing process, we managed to discover many new ideas for her
paper. . . . For instance, when we were working on a
sentence about how Easy Cheese had a bad after-taste,
I asked her if she knew this from personal experience. She didn't. . . . I recommended that she taste
it herself and write about the personal experience.
I wouldn't have asked the student if she had tasted
Easy Cheese if we hadn't been carefully examining each
sentence while editing.

Realizing that Brendan has a new theory to share with other tutors, I can
only add in my weekly letter: "There's the beginning of an article right there,
including what you say about how at first you tried developing ideas without
going to the sentence level." It's interesting to notice how Brendan's "edivision," as he's begun calling it, takes him back to what he found so useful in
Nancy Welch's class, taking sentences that "lacked thick, compelling substance" and "reflecting on these sentences [to] change my whole paper."

My Own Questions

As I thought more about my role in the letter exchange, Brendan's questions became my own questions. Indeed, they are questions appropriate for anyone
considering setting up a letter exchange with writing tutors or with students doing independent studies or internships for that matter.

Why do I want to exchange letters with tutors? Initially assessment was on
my mind. If tutors were to be graded on their tutoring, I needed to know what
their sessions were like. I had tried videotaping sessions, but found this practice too intrusive. I read log notes, but tutors try to be descriptive and objective
in their log notes, knowing students can have copies sent to their instructors. I
knew my best information about how the tutoring was going would be coming
from the letters. Still, a more important answer to the why question was that I
wanted to create a relationship of "taking care," of mentoring, and to learn with
and from the tutors.

What knowledge and attitudes do I bring to the exchange? Like Brendan,
I have learned that it's not as much the knowledge I bring, though my many
years of tutoring and teaching are of course useful, so much as an attitude, a

basic trust in tutors' own thinking. That trust provides an answer to the next question, How do I position myself in the letter exchange? Just as the tutors usually choose to position themselves as peers rather than authorities when working with student writers, in our letter exchange I like to establish a peer relationship with tutors, though we all know it's not that simple. I'm not a peer in that I have much more experience; I'm not a peer in status; I'm certainly not a peer in that I have to give their tutoring and writing a grade. But I am a peer in that I genuinely respect tutors' ideas and am part of a relationship in which we learn together. And the letter exchange, along with the tutor-training classroom, is the perfect place to demonstrate that respect and create a space for collaborative learning.

This brings me to the last question: what theory grows out of a letter exchange such as ours? For me, the theory suggested is that close attention to sessions, reflection on sessions, conversations about sessions provide a vehicle for learning—about connecting with student writers, about these writers' learning styles and writing processes, about strategies for advancing a draft. Like "edivision," this way of reading and focusing, this looking closely in order to see more broadly, can add "thick, compelling substance" to our thinking about teaching and tutoring.

Works Cited

Bruffee, K. 1984. "Peer Tutoring and the 'Conversation of Mankind.'" In *Writing Centers: Theory and Administration,* ed. G. Olson, 3–15. Urbana, IL: NCTE.

Kail, H., and J. Trimbur. 1987. "The Politics of Peer Tutoring." *The Writing Center Journal* 11.1–2: 5–12.

Lucey, B. 1998. "Editing Revisited." National Conference on Peer Tutoring in Writing. SUNY Plattsburgh, Plattsburgh, NY.

North, S. 1984. "The Idea of a Writing Center." *College English* 46.5: 433–46.

Welch, N. 1997. *Getting Restless: Rethinking Revision in Writing Instruction.* Portsmouth, NH: Boynton/Cook.

Afterword

Questions About Teaching with Letters
Toby Fulwiler

As much as we believe in the power of letters to help students and teachers advance writing and learning, we also know they don't work every time, nor in every setting, nor for everyone. Sometimes, instructors who value letter writing themselves are unable to convince students of their value. Other times, instructors who find letters effective in one course find them ineffective in another. And, finally, some instructors and/or students who exchange class letters find them more bothersome than profitable. At the same time, a decade of practice has convinced me that there are reasonable solutions to some of the problems associated with letter assignments. Following are some answers to frequently asked questions about teaching with letters.

Do letter exchanges work in any course? If you're a college English teacher whose primary business is exploring and encouraging written expression, letters can play provocative and varied roles in any writing or literature class— to which we hope the chapters in this book attest. In some classes the letters are assigned as supplementary writing, supporting larger writing assignments (Dinitz, Fulwiler, Schnell, Jersen) while in other classes letters become a primary assignment in themselves (Stephany, Orth, Keidaisch). Whether letters work in your particular course depends on what you want to accomplish. I believe they work in any university course—English or otherwise—where informal communication would help advance the goals and learning objectives of that course. The logistics of such exchanges would depend on how large the class is and how often it meets.

How do I get students to take letter assignments seriously? Students take seriously the assignments that their instructors take seriously. When students don't take letters seriously, it's probably because they sense they are not important, that they're not an essential part of class, or that they don't count. If you want students to value letter assignments, you need to move them from the back burner, one way or another, to the front burner. If you introduce letters on your syllabus, take class time to explain how they work, attend to them in class, and count them in some way, serious students will take them seriously. Some of the strategies the authors of this book have found successful include: posing specific questions letters might address; answering questions that student letters pose; reading provocative letters aloud in class; reserving class time for letter writing, sharing, and responding; asking that letters be included in writing portfolios; collecting end-of-term "annotated editions of the letters," or counting them by either quantitative or qualitative grading.

Some instructors grade student letters while others simply give credit— what's the difference? How you weigh and assess letters all depends on why you are assigning them, who is writing to whom, and in what spirit you end up reading them. For instance, if students write letters directly to you, a written response, individual (Dinitz) or collective (Fulwiler) showing that you've read and thought about the letter easily substitutes for formal assessment. Or, if students exchange letters with each other, with copies to you, perhaps students may receive credit or points for simply making the exchange. In these examples, the letters function as "writing-to-learn" assignments, so that part of the reason for the writing is to help the letter writers explore ideas for themselves rather than demonstrate completed learning to someone else. When you treat letter writing as you would journal writing or freewriting, you encourage exploration and experimentation, and downplay the specificity of qualitative assessment— grades. (See the chapters by Dickerson, Dinitz, Fulwiler, Stewart, and Jersen for examples of writing-to-learn letters that are not graded.)

In contrast, if letters are assigned to reveal specific student knowledge, understanding, or skill via an informal medium, grades that reflect the quality of the response are appropriate. (See chapters by Baruth, Keidaisch, Orth, Stephany, and Schnell for examples of graded letter assignments.)

If students write letters to me, how can I possibly respond to them all in one class, let alone several classes at once. I teach no classes small enough in which I could correspond with every student in class on a weekly basis. Instead, in classes where I ask individual students to write weekly letters to me, I write what I call *collective letters* back. That is, I read all student letters, noting interesting questions and concerns; then I write a letter to the whole class (Dear Classmates) in which I repeat and address the student questions and concerns; then I deliver a copy of this letter to the class at our next meeting. However, some instructors of small classes switch from other forms of responses to student learning (quizzes, paper comments, or conferences) to letters, thereby trading one form of response for another, but taking no more time to do so (Dinitz, Keidaisch, Stephany). Still other instructors eavesdrop on student-student letter writing and do not formally respond at all until a final evaluation is due (Stewart, Schnell).

However, if you're going to collect letters from several classes or a large class, it only makes sense to stagger your collecting, so you only have to read a manageable number at a given time. For instance, when I have two classes at a time exchanging letters with me, I alternate due days or weeks to make it easier on myself. Colleagues who teach classes of more than, say, fifty usually stagger letter due dates, receiving letters from half, a third, or a quarter of the class each week, which lightens the instructor reading load as well as the student writing load, yet still guarantees that the instructor keeps in touch with class questions and concerns. When students write letters to each other, of course, instructor responses are not expected.

How can I make sure students write letters about academic, not personal matters? Make it clear on your syllabus that assigned letters address course matters. Ask that letters written address 1) issues that arise during class discussion, 2) ideas and questions from the assigned readings, and 3) personal matters when they intersect with course content. However, sometimes letters serve learning in more oblique ways, such as providing a place for students, by writing, to let off steam, organize their lives, or get rid of distracting "noise" (Stephany). Of course, students, like any letter writers, may choose to share more private thoughts as well, but that's a matter of personal choice. I think, however, that if the letters are addressed to you, their instructor and an authority figure, they carefully control what they choose to share, understanding that the assignment requests a candid exchange of ideas rather than details of private lives. At the same time, when students write letters to each other, you can suggest but not control the topics they choose to write about.

When do journals work better than letters? Some of us who collaborated upon this book actually assign *both* letters and journals in the hope that these more relaxed modes of writing will encourage a more honest exploration of ideas than do formal papers and examinations. When I assign both journals and letters in the same class, I collect only the letters, trusting that the journals, which are used for both in-class freewriting and out-of-class pondering, will be kept in good faith and that the ideas that deserve to be made public will find their way into the letters that students share with me.

Sometimes, however, the addition of an audience to exploratory writing—which is the main difference between letters and journals—compromises the honesty or depth with which students try out ideas or raise questions. Journals, because they are written primarily for the writer, work better when public sharing is less important than private reasoning, reacting, and figuring out—I write in my own journal several times a week to reason my way through my life; I would not want to share most of what I write with any audience but myself. When students are working on projects or doing internships, daily journal writing would make more sense than equally frequent letter writing.

What specific guidelines do you actually give students when you assign letters? Most of the chapter writers in this book describe the specific guidelines that accompany their assignments, some of which include fictive purposes such as letter poems, imitation eighteenth-century epistolary exchanges, and role playing. However, in the case of letters meant to be authentic real-time exchanges between and among faculty and students, the following general guidelines may be useful:

Function. A letter communicates thoughts on a writer's mind to a specific audience, usually the course instructor and/or other members of the class. As such, its general function is to explore ideas from the course by expressing opinions or asking questions. The medium of the informal letter is chosen to promote more candid exchanges of ideas than more formal written assignments do, often with the further intention of helping class members become more familiar with each other, thereby making for more relaxed and open class meetings. However, look at the several specific goals articulated by chapter writers in *The Letter Book:* 1) to get to know their students better (most of the chapter writers in this book), 2) to create a positive learning environment (most of the chapter writers), 3) to advance formal writing projects (Dinitz, Fulwiler), 4) to assess student understanding and growth (Stephany, Keidaisch), 5) to facilitate collaborative work (Dickerson, Schnell), 6) to learn literary genres (Orth, Baruth), 7) to rehearse professional discourse (Jersen), and 8) to create stronger classroom community (Fulwiler, Stewart).

Voice and Style. School letters, like real-world letters, are usually written in an informal style, in the writer's speaking voice, and include first-person pronouns, colloquial expressions, contractions, and humor. While there are no absolute rules that govern the voice and style of letters, they commonly sound like a person's conversational speech written down. In letters, unlike formal paper assignments, most instructors ignore matters of spelling, punctuation, and grammar, emphasizing instead the content of the ideas and concerns rather than the correctness of the product.

Form. Letters follow three main conventions: 1) they are addressed to a specific audience, 2) they are signed by the author, and 3) they are dated. Beyond that, letters may assume any one of a number of forms, including the formality of memos and business letters, the informality of personal notes and friendly letters, or the artifice of poetry and fiction.

Frequency. It all depends. That's the only complete answer, since how often you ask students to write depends upon your purpose in assigning letters in the first place. Some chapter writers here assign letters on a weekly basis (Dinitz, Keidaish), on a weekly basis for a limited time (Stewart, Fulwiler, Jersen); at regular intervals throughout the semester (Stephany, Schnell), at irregular intervals (Dickerson), or as specific assignments for a short period of time (Orth, Baruth). While some of us prefer frequent, regular, and predictable exchanges, whether between students and instructor, or students and each other, others schedule more limited exchanges to accomplish other goals. It all depends.

About the Contributors

Philip Baruth is an Associate Professor at the University of Vermont. A specialist in eighteenth-century literature, he is the editor of *Introducing Charlotte Charke* (University of Illinois Press, 1998), a collection dedicated to the life and work of Charke, Colley Cibber's youngest daughter and a much-underestimated actress and autobiographer.

Mary Jane Dickerson, Associate Professor of English at the University of Vermont, is the co-author of *Writer's Guide To History,* the author of literary criticism such as "Women in *Go Down, Moses,*" and has had poems in magazines such as *Harper's.* She teaches courses in American literature and writing autobiography.

Sue Dinitz has been teaching writing courses at the University of Vermont for the past twenty years, spending some of those years also directing the UVM Writing Center and training UVM's graduate teaching fellows. She currently co-directs the Writing Center with Jean Kiedaisch, and has published articles in *Writing Center Journal, Writing Lab Newsletter,* the *Journal of Teaching Writing,* and *Language and Learning Across the Disciplines.*

Toby Fulwiler is a professor of English who has directed the writing program at the University of Vermont since 1983, where he teaches introductory and advanced writing classes. His most recent books include *The Journal Book for Teachers of At-Risk Writers, The Journal Book for Teachers of Professional and Technical Programs,* and second editions of *The Working Writer, College Writing,* and *College Writer's Reference.*

Traci Jersen received her Master of Arts in English from the University of Vermont in 1998, where she was a Graduate Teaching Fellow and taught introductory writing classes. She is now a writer and editor in New York City.

Jean Kiedaisch is director of Vermont's Learning Cooperative, an academic support center, and has taught composition at UVM since 1980. She directed the UVM Writing Center for nine years, publishing articles in *The Writing Center Journal* and *The Writing Lab Newsletter,* served as co-director of FOCUS, a program for first-year students, and taught first-year seminars for five years.

Ghita Orth teaches poetry and creative-writing courses at the University of Vermont. Her book of poems, *The Music Of What Happens,* was published by Saturday Press as winner of its Eileen W. Barnes Award. She has published poetry in *Poem, Dark Horse, Appalachia, New England Review,* and other journals, and was a co-editor of *Angles of Vision* (McGraw-Hill), a textbook for introductory literature courses. She has also written, with David Huddle and Allen Shepherd, *About These Stories* (McGraw-Hill), a fiction text for creative writing classes.

Lisa Schnell, a Canadian by birth, tried out an American identity from 1985–90 while doing her Ph.D. at Princeton University. She officially immigrated in 1992 when she took a job as an Assistant Professor of English at The University of Vermont where she teaches Renaissance drama and poetry, the Bible as literature, and critical theory. A recent recipient of an Open Society Humanities Fellowship, she was also honored in 1998–99 as UVM's Graduate Teacher of the Year.

William Stephany teaches medieval literature and drama courses in the University of Vermont's English department. He contributed to the department's collaboratively produced books, *Reading, Writing, and the Study of Literature* and *Angles of Vision,* and he is co-editor, with James Howe, of *The McGraw-Hill Book of Drama.*

Karen Stewart is a faculty member in The Writing Program at Beloit College, where she teaches first-year composition and a peer writing consultant course, and coordinates writing center work. Before joining The Writing Program, she taught at Southern Vermont College and the University of Vermont. She frequently leads workshops on writing in the disciplines and in first-year seminars. She spends as much time as possible at her home in Vermont where she works in her garden, cooks with wood, and enjoys her family.